Reincarnation
Unnecessary

Reincarnation Unnecessary

Based on the Edgar Cayce Readings

By Violet M. Shelley

A.R.E. PRESS • VIRGINIA BEACH • VIRGINIA

Printed in the U.S.A.

CONTENTS

Reincarnation Unnecessary

Chapter One
THE WHEEL OF CHANGE

Who toiled a slave may come anew a Prince
For gentle worthiness and merit won;
Who ruled a King may wander earth in rags
For things done and undone . . .

Only, while turns this wheel invisible,
No pause, no peace, no staying-place can be;
Who mounts will fall, who falls may mount; the spokes
go round unceasingly!

The Light of Asia
Edwin Arnold

When, in 1925, Edgar Cayce learned that he had in his altered state of consciousness mentioned reincarnation, he was both astounded and perplexed. Deeply concerned most of his adult life that his mysterious psychic ability might be misused, he wondered whether this intrusion of an Eastern concept, unfamiliar to him in his conscious state, was evidence of evil forces at work. Educated eventually by his own readings (as his psychic dissertations were called) on the subject, Cayce went on to give twenty-five hundred readings which outlined individuals' past lives in the earth, describing patterns from those lives which influenced the present personality. A sincerely religious man steeped in the Christian faith and the Bible, Cayce was to find that there was nothing in the concept of reincarnation which was inconsistent with his Christian beliefs or which would be construed as contradictory to them. Those who study the implications inherent in the concept are inclined to agree that the theory offers both answers and explanations for many hitherto perplexing questions not answered by orthodoxy.

From the vantage point of time one can look back over the years at the consternation that the introduction of this idea caused Edgar Cayce and those around him. Here was a group of people who had for years witnessed a strange phenomenon: a man who could lie down before them, seemingly go to sleep, and after being given a suggestion, comment on the internal or psychological condition of a total stranger who might be thousands of miles away. He demonstrated that from this altered state of consciousness he could trace the physical activities of an individual or describe the clothes the person was wearing. On numerous occasions he commented on specifics of the locale where the person was. In the midst of this diverse activity he was known to correct his secretary's spelling or tune into her thoughts—all without moving, without opening his eyes, without waking from his trance state. Many times upon waking at the end of a reading, Cayce would report a dream that he had just had, a dream that had nothing whatever to do with what he had just been saying. Later a reading would be taken to get an interpretation of that dream. Those around Cayce were familiar with the accuracy and reliability of the information that came through him and accepted with equanimity both the fact that his mind was capable of all this disparate activity and the fact that some part of his consciousness was able to move with unhindered ease through time and space. Yet these same people were at first dumbfounded at the casual mention of someone having lived before. They, too, with Cayce, came to accept the comforting logic of the concept, as do many many thousands of people today.

To some people, however, the idea of having lived before and having to live again is still unsettling. Lack of information or vague fears often close their minds, yet all around in nature are regular demonstrations of reincarnation in the cycles of death and rebirth that we all take for granted. The fragile daffodil that blooms in the spring is one such example. The flower lives its short life until its glorious yellow fades, turns brown, and withers away. The daffodil is dead, but the next April, another daffodil opens its petals to the sun. Nobody claims that it is the same daffodil, but it is an expression of life from the same bulb. The deciduous trees, green in the summer, brightly colored in the fall, lose their leaves in the winter, and appear dead. The next spring, delicate buds appear and with them new life. Rudyard Kipling wrote, "He who wasted not a leaf or tree, Would He have squandered souls?"

The Latin word *carnis,* meaning flesh, is the root of the word reincarnation as it is of many other English words—carnal, carnage, carnivore, carnival, carnelian. The flower, carnation, originally pink, was so named because it was flesh colored. Reincarnation literally means "in the flesh again." Coined to describe a soul process, it means that the soul is back in a body again. In similar vein, the word discarnate describes a soul without a body. There are a number of other words in the language that have almost the same meaning as

2

reincarnation, and although they are sometimes used interchangeably there are slightly different nuances attendant and they are less precise in meaning. Some of these are *metempsychosis, palingenesis, pre-existence* and *transcorporation.* Somerset Maugham used *transmigration* as synonymous with reincarnation, but that word has become so closely associated with the belief that human souls can be born into animal bodies that it is no longer considered to be an accurate synonym. This latter is considered by reincarnationists to be false and a complete reversal of natural evolutionary processes.

It its very simplest form, the concept of reincarnation encompasses the belief that the soul of man is divine and eternal—its natural evolution is toward its eventual return to the Divine Source from which it came. This perfection can be obtained only through the process of rebirth. In other words, we have lived before and we will live again until we have learned to identify with our own divine reality instead of materiality. Nothing is lost in these series of rebirths. All that has been gained remains a permanent part of the soul's individuality. Lessons failed will be met again and again until they are learned. All that one does is returned in kind, an immutable law referred to as karma. Reincarnation, aptly referred to as the continuity of life, is a way of defining the soul's immortality and is a demonstration of the Creator's loving justice.

It is the idea of justice that starts many people searching outside of orthodoxy for answers. To define God as Love and then lay all tragedy and misfortune at His door as His *will* seems eminently contradictory. We are taught that all men are created equal but we don't have to look very far to see that some are more equal than others. We are told that at the end of life we will be judged and at that time get our just deserts—heaven or hell, lolling with the righteous or burning eternally with the damned. A thinking person begins to wonder whether there are not some gray areas rather than this black or white theory. One child is born physically handicapped, the thirteenth unwanted, underfed child in a sharecropper's shack. Another child is born with sound mind and body to parents who will love him, protect him, educate him and give him every possible advantage. The first hasn't had a chance from the start and, considering the dire circumstances, will have little opportunity to rise above his environment. Would a loving and just Creator judge these two by the same standards? We are taught that good is rewarded and evil punished, that honesty is the best policy and that crime does not pay. Observation often suggests the very opposite and one can cite instances where crime has paid very well indeed. Where is the justice?

A belief in reincarnation returns to us a sense of justice and allows us to make sense out of much we see. Rather than laying blame on a stern and whimsical God for the inequalities we see around us, we now can see people in a world of cause and effect. According to this theory, each of us is born into the best possible circumstances for the soul to learn its lessons. Souls are indeed created equal. The unequal circumstances in which they find themselves are the result of earlier causes, earlier choices. The law of karma, or reaping what we sow, is operating. There are no innocent victims. We have built what we are and we are building what we will become. As for the correctness of seemingly unrewarded good deeds and profitable crime—a more thorough view will show that justice does prevail. Like the law of gravity, the law works whether one believes in it or not. One reaps what he has sown in deed, word and thought; if not in this life, in one to come.

Acceptance of the concept of reincarnation takes a crutch away from us; we can no longer blame anyone else for the positions in which we find ourselves. We cannot blame our parents, our teachers, our spouses or God. We are the result of our choices, our actions and our thoughts in the past. God is love and God is just. It is that loving justice that allows us all the time we need to recognize the divine spark within us and all the time we need to start on our return to Him. Instead of being incompatible with Christianity, the belief tends to emphasize it because the teachings of the Christ must be put into application if we are to realize our destiny.

If this is so, people ask, why is reincarnation not discussed in the Bible? A number of theories have been advanced in an attempt to answer that question. One is that reincarnation was always an esoteric doctrine taught only to initiates. Josephus reports that it was a belief held by the Essenes. It was also taught by Plato and Pythagoras. Another theory was put forth which suggested that eleven references to reincarnation were deliberately removed from the Bible by order of the emperor Justinian. However, scholars attest that there are manuscripts extant of scriptures which long pre-date Justinian and that they are as lacking in reincarnation teachings as later versions. A theory postulates that the belief in reincarnation had such wide acceptance at the time of Jesus, that it was simply assumed. A number of passages that imply reincarnation seem to support the third theory and make it seem the most plausible.

Matthew 16:13-14: "When Jesus came into the coasts of Caesarea Philippi, he asked his disciples, saying, Whom do men say that I, the Son of man, am? And they said, Some say that thou art John the Baptist; some, Elias; and others,

Jeremias, or one of the prophets."

Mark 6:15-16: "Others said, That it is Elias. And others said, That it is a prophet, or as one of the prophets. But when Herod heard thereof, he said, It is John whom I beheaded: he is risen from the dead."

John 9:1-3: "And as Jesus passed by, he saw a man which was blind from birth. And his disciples asked him saying, Master, who did sin, this man, or his parents that he was born blind?"

All of these are open references to reincarnation and in none of the instances did Jesus speak out against the belief. The following verses indicate that Jesus Himself was convinced that John the Baptist was Elijah reincarnated. Some versions say Elias which is simply the Greek form of the name.

Matthew 11:11-15: "Among them that are born of women there hath not risen a greater than John the Baptist ... For all the prophets and the law prophesied until John. And if ye will receive it, this is Elias, which was for to come. He that hath ears to hear let him hear."

Matthew 17:9-13: "And as they came down from the mountain Jesus charged them saying, Tell the vision to no man, until the Son of man be risen again from the dead.

"And his disciples asked him, saying, Why then say the scribes that Elias must first come? And Jesus answered and said unto them, Elias truly shall first come, and restore all things. But I say unto you, That Elias is come already, and they knew him not, but have done unto him whatsoever they listed. Likewise shall also the Son of man suffer of them.

"Then the disciples understood that he spake unto them of John the Baptist."

Although modern day Judaism espouses no belief in the theory of reincarnation, ancient writing in the Kabala discusses it in detail. *Reincarnation in World Thought* by Head and Cranston offers quite a number of selections that illustrate this thinking. While perhaps not the best example, one of my favorites is this: "If a man be niggardly whether in a financial or a spiritual regard, giving nothing of his money to the poor or not imparting of his knowledge to the ignorant, he shall be punished by transmigration into a woman." In a footnote the authors describe this as "an arrogant error" perpetuated also by Hinduism. Later in the excerpt the writer says, "Some times the souls of pious Jews pass by metempsychosis into Gentiles, in order that they may plead on behalf of Israel and treat them kindly." (*Yalkut Reubeni*)

This quotation from *The Zohar* may be more definitive:

"The souls must re-enter the absolute substance when they have emerged. But to accomplish this end they must develop all

5

the perfections, the germ of which is planted in them; and if they have not fulfilled this condition during one life, they must commence another, a third, and so forth, until they have acquired the condition which fits them for reunion with God."

That reincarnation is a belief with a background in all of the world's major religions and one held by many hundreds of the world's greatest thinkers of all time is overwhelmingly evidenced by the two anthologies by Head and Cranston, *Reincarnation: An East-West Anthology,* 1961, and *Reincarnation in World Thought,* 1967. Here in addition to excerpts from a wide assortment of religious writings are selections from scientists, philosophers, psychologists, poets, novelists, artists, inventors, ministers from all over the world. Sir Arthur Conan Doyle, Tennyson, Browning, Kipling, Maugham, Masefield, Pasternak, Lindbergh, Schopenhauer, Hugo, Tolstoy, Whitman, Ibsen, Dostoevsky, Huxley, Einstein, Jung—the list could go on and on. While this doesn't offer scientific proof of the theory, it certainly does suggest that believing in the concept puts you in some very erudite company.

If ever scientifically acceptable proof is to come it will probably be through the meticulous research of Ian Stevenson, M.D., of the University of Virginia or someone as thoroughly painstaking and objective as he is. In 1966 Dr. Stevenson published a monograph entitled *Twenty Cases Suggestive of Reincarnation,* a representative sample of several hundred cases he and his colleagues had personally investigated of the six hundred they had listed at the time. In the years that have intervened since that publication Dr. Stevenson has not stopped traveling around the world investigating claimed memories of past lives, and it is impossible to say how many thousands of cases are on his list now.

The cases evaluated are all instances where a child spontaneously remembered a previous life, many with vivid detail. Dr. Stevenson was able to interview most of them and their families within a fairly short period of time after they first started talking about it. In addition to the stories he has listed the items the child remembered, the names of the informants and the names of people who were able to verify the items. The book makes fascinating reading for anyone interested in a look at reincarnation from a scientific angle. Dr. Stevenson states "that *some* of the cases do much more than suggest reincarnation; they seem to me to furnish considerable evidence for it."

Some of these spontaneous recollections of previous personalities started when the children were as young as one and a half. Many gradually diminished but a few persisted. The average duration was seven years. Almost all of the cases appeared in ethnic groups that either accept or are familiar with the concept of reincarnation. In a number of instances the previous personality had predicted his return to a specific family. One old Tlingit Indian not only announced to his nephew's wife that he would be born to her as her son, but also said that she would recognize him by his scars. With that he pointed to surgical scars. Eighteen months after the death of the old man a boy was born to the niece with birthmarks in the predicted places. Dr. Stevenson reports that one in particular closely resembles an operative scar. This same child at the age of thirteen months refused to be called by the name his parents had given him and identified himself as "Kahkody," the tribal name of the old man who had died.

A characteristic that these cases have in common is that they were all fairly quick returns to life of the previous personality. This, of course, is what makes them capable of being studied and authenticated and consequently scientifically acceptable. It should not be inferred that all souls make such quick reappearances, because, according to other writings, this is determined by desire and will.

Dr. Stevenson found patterns within the personalities of these cases that could not have been inherited or acquired in the present life. There were informational patterns about people and places known to the deceased personality and not available to the present one. There were behavioral patterns which included skills, mannerisms, fears, special likings, and aversions. There are also specific physical patterns such as the birthmarks already mentioned.

And so, from Hinduism through Judaism and on into Christianity, comes reincarnation—a subject for 20th century scientific study.

Chapter Two
ECHOES FROM THE PAST

Was I a Samurai renowned,
Two-sworded, fierce, immense of bow?
A histrion angular and profound?
A priest? A porter? . . .
Ballade of a Toyokuni Colour Print
William Ernest Henley

That the past may sometimes be heard resoundingly in the present seems amply demonstrated by the incidence throughout history of child prodigies. There are many documented cases of children who have shown exceptional abilities in music, in foreign languages, at chess, in mathematics. I knew one such six-year-old boy whose brain seemed to be a lightning calculator for complicated mathematical problems, but that was long before I had ever heard of reincarnation. He, like many other child prodigies, came from a family whose brothers and sisters showed no similar aptitude although their heredity and environment were the same.

Mozart wrote a sonata when he was four and an opera when he was seven. He played the violin with his father's string group without any training when he was about six. Young Chopin soon surpassed his piano teacher's limited abilities. Eventually he was to be taught harmony and composition at the conservatory, but he was basically a self-taught pianist whose technique and skills were so completely different that many of his études and preludes were written in order to teach those difficult techniques. Chopin, Johann Hummel and Yehudi Menuhin all gave public concerts by the age of eleven. A precocious German child, Christian Heinecken (1721-25) spoke Latin and French by the age of three and was able to give public demonstrations of historical, geographical and Biblical knowledge. Sir William Hamilton started to learn Hebrew at the age of three and at the age of thirteen could speak thirteen languages, including Persian, Arabic, Sanskrit, Hindustani and Malay.

Why one child should hop up on a piano stool and begin

playing or composing while most of his contemporaries are contented to kick their blocks around cannot be easily explained without a belief in reincarnation. Plato held that "knowledge which is easily acquired is that which the enduring self had in an earlier life, so that it flows back easily." The Cayce readings concur that no talent or skill is lost from life to life, although some may be temporarily ignored or forgotten. In the case of child prodigies, it well may be that their memories are open to previously developed abilities.

Another instance of an echo from the past is the story of an Italian couple, Captain and Mrs. Battista and their daughter, Blanche. When their child was born, the Battistas hired a French-speaking Swiss nurse who, in the ensuing years, taught the child a French lullaby. Unfortunately, the child died at a very young age and the nurse returned to Switzerland. Three years later Mrs. Battista became pregnant. In her fourth month she dreamed of her dead child who said that she was coming back. The child was born in February, 1906, and at her mother's insistence was given the name, Blanche. She resembled the first child in every way. When she was six years old she began to sing in perfect French the cradle song taught to the first Blanche. The nurse had been gone for nine years and, because of the unhappy associations with the song, the parents had neither sung it nor taught it to her. When asked how she knew it, she replied simply that she knew it "out of my own head." Her father, who had been skeptical, concluded that the only possible explanation was rebirth.

An experience which occurs rather commonly is one known as the *déjà vu* experience. Literally translated it means "already seen" and consists of a sense of familiarity with a place never seen before. Dante Gabriel Rossetti wrote:

I have been here before,
But when or how I cannot tell;
I know the grass beyond the door,
The sweet keen smell.

The deep feeling of familiarity with a strange place, scene or situation may or may not be the nudging of a memory from a past life. Some of these occurrences have been proven to be simply the coming to conscious recall of something subliminally impressed on the mind in this life. One such instance reported by Dr. Ian Stevenson was of an English army officer and his wife who, while touring a part of the country where neither had ever been before, came upon a wayside pool which they both thought they recognized. They felt that they certainly must have lived in the area in a previous life.

9

However, upon their return to London they visited an art gallery to which they had been before. There they saw a painting of a wayside pool which they had both forgotten. According to the Cayce readings, we often preview forthcoming events in our dreams and some *déjà vu* experiences truly were "seen before," but seen in a dream rather than in a past existence.

Some recorded *déjà vu* experiences are more than just a feeling of familiarity and the person having the experience is able to supply descriptive details of which he could have no previous knowledge. These are paranormal and cannot be explained other than as valid echoes from the past.

One experience reported by Dr. Leslie Weatherhead in his printed lecture, "The Case for Reincarnation," was of a small boy whose mother had reported a number of such incidents. One time they were visiting some caves in Guernsey which had been used years before as prisons for French soldiers. The boy said that there was another cave where a young man had been walled in, and that he had watched it being done. He also gave the name of the prisoner. At first the authorities denied the existence of such a cave, but finally a door was found which had been bricked up. In the cave was found the skeleton of a man, and the archives proved that the name the boy had given was correct.

Many of the *déjà vu* experiences seem fragmentary, such as knowledge of a town or place where one has never been and descriptions of the existence of a peculiar room in an inaccessible part of a ruined castle—echoes only. However, to one German housewife the experience opened up her immediate past life during World War II and frightened her. Driving with her husband through an unfamiliar province of Germany she recognized the area and suddenly details of her past life as well as her name came to her mind. The tavern owner in the village verified the details and when he described the tragic way the child Maria had died, she relived the whole accident. The horror of reliving being kicked to death by a horse sent her fleeing from the village without attempting to contact the still-living brother of the previous personality. It convinced her, however, of the reality of rebirth. The case was reported in a German weekly and in Martin Ebon's *Reincarnation in the Twentieth Century*.

The children investigated by Dr. Stevenson remembered who and where they had been in their past lives. They remembered parents, events and friends. Observers were able to recognize patterns brought over from the previous life. Many people wish that they could do likewise. The concept of reincarnation while dousing the fires of hell and relieving God of a scapegoat position raises questions of its own and tosses a few temptations in the path. One of those is the Cosmic Casting Game in which the players choose a famous person or a great personality, identify with it and get lost in the limbo of yesteryear. Meanwhile, back in the twentieth century, the dishes and laundry pile up while Catherine the Great stares out of the widow preparing for a ball in Petersburg. Pseudopsychics are fond of doling out well-known characters from history as previous incarnations—after all, it's a great ego builder and who can say them nay? At one time some years ago we knew six different people all claiming to be the incarnation of the same apostle. It is just this kind of fantasizing that often makes the entire idea of rebirth suspect.

Another temptation which, like the former, will be a primrose path only to those who haven't examined all of the aspects of the concept is procrastination. Reincarnation is, after all, one way of looking at eternity—eternity that stretches into the past and into the future. For a truly dedicated procastinator, that is extremely good news; there is not only a tomorrow but endless tomorrows. Things do not have to be accomplished in one lifetime; there are lifetimes without end. But that is to miss the point. Each of us, the Cayce readings tell us, is in the best possible place to learn what we need to learn. If we defer that learning, it is highly possible that things will be much more difficult for us in the next life. Talents and abilities that are neglected or unused atrophy just as do unused limbs.

Both of these temptations, like all temptations that hinder souls on the spiritual path, are simply facets of the one great temptation: self. The only barrier between the Creator and the divine soul of man is the self-conscious mind. Every thought and act of self-concern and self-indulgence builds that barrier stronger and delays the soul's progress. Consequently, if we have an interest in knowing who we were and where we have been, it might be well to examine first our purpose in wanting to know. If the knowledge can aid us to develop our abilities and overcome deep-seated problems, the search might be valid.

In the general discussion section at the end of his book, Dr. Stevenson states that each of the children he investigated often felt, or the behavior suggested, a continuity of personality with the person who had died. Just as in our own lives we know ourselves to be very different personalities at fifty than we were at thirty or twenty or ten, we also know that we are the same person. Our memories provide the continuity for us. The Cayce readings maintain that the subconscious mind is the storehouse of all of our memories from this and past lives and that often we act on those memories without being consciously aware that we do so. In this way our talents are really memories of a skill we had in previous lives. Our intuitive choices in decor, dress, jewelry, food, music often reflect past lives. An examination of them can give us many clues. Our emotional natures are the result of our experiences in the earth. As for the problems we must overcome and the lessons we ought to learn, we need to look no further than that which we face every day. Our own patterns will emerge very easily.

We can hear echoes from the past when we know how to listen for them. In a dream we may experience having another identity and acting out a scene in another time and place. Some situation in our conscious waking life may have triggered this information. In a *déjà vu* experience, an overwhelming sense of familiarity may convince us that we have already witnessed a place or situation that is totally new to us. These experiences are much more common than many people think. Researchers have documented hundreds.

During his lifetime Edgar Cayce gave more than twenty-five-hundred readings for people in which he described past lives in the earth that influenced the present personality. The readings describe only a few past existences for each individual but this does not mean these were the only lives the person had lived. According to the readings, only a limited number of previous sojourns were influencing the current experience. Results attributed to previous existences included physical problems, emotional entanglements, talents, skills, and even personalities. The readings carefully adhered to a philosophy they espoused: magnify the virtues and minimize the faults. They were to guide, help and encourage the people who asked for them. Dr. Gina Cerminara's books, *Many Mansions* and *The World Within,* are fascinating and detailed studies of these readings. They show how people get their own patterns started and keep repeating them. The patterns extend to groups of people who keep incarnating together for weal or for woe—to work in loving harmony or battle it out another time.

The concept of reincarnation seems to promise glamor, but a careful study of these readings dispels this illusion. Like a patient teacher, the readings frequently reiterate the message that souls were created in the beginning, *in the image of the Father,* meaning in *spirit.* The reality of man, that which exists throughout eternity, is his spirit. Man's soul is composed of spirit, mind and will. Mind and spirit are part of the Creator. Man's will is his birthright, a gift. Man's use of his will got him entangled in the earth, and only its proper use will make possible an understanding of his true nature. Eventually we will realize we are here to learn the lessons set for us by our own willfulness. It is difficult to see how any of us would want to feel a great amount of pride for our entanglements. Our condition is the same as the Prodigal Son's—separated by choice from the Father, wasting the inheritance of free will, entering a pigsty called "Earth." We can look forward to fulfilling the rest of that parable: when the son decided to return home, his father saw him coming (a long way off) and came to meet him.

The wheel has long been a symbol of reincarnation in phrases such as: the "Wheel of the Law" and the "Wheel of Change." The story of Ixion bound to the wheel is the story of the soul of man entrapped in a pattern of cyclic return. Are we all bound forever to this wheel of return, incarnation following incarnation with no surcease? "There are many entities in the spirit plane that have not chosen to come back to earth," said Edgar Cayce at the conclusion of one reading. His next few words were inaudible, but he went on to add, "There are many about us now."

They had not *chosen* to come back. Here is a clear statement that the soul's free will is not lost when it sheds its material body. Here also is the indication of the reality of a plane which is not the same as the three-dimensional one that our conscious minds accept.

Reincarnation is necessary for the soul's pilgrimage back to the Father. The concept implies that we have all the time we need to learn to overcome the material plane and the attachments and desires that have long pulled us back to it. It is only here in the earth plane that we can work out our emotional problems, our relationships with others, learn to love others, learn to forgive, learn to use our daily choices to make our will one with the will of the Father. We know our problems, the chains that bind us to the wheel, and we wonder how long we will keep bouncing in and out of the same old situations. One man having a reading from Mr. Cayce posed the question: "How long will I need to reincarnate?" The answer was, "How long will you require?"

Some twelve hundred people received life readings from Edgar Cayce. Of these, eighteen were told that when their lives ended they *might* choose not to return. These readings are indexed under the heading: *Reincarnation: Unnecessary.*

We have explored some of the aspects of reincarnation as necessary; let us see what the Cayce readings say about it being unnecessary.

Chapter Three
PATTERNS AND PROMISES

Our deeds still travel with us from afar
And what we have been makes us what we are.
George Eliot

Although some of the index cards under *Reincarnation: Unnecessary* refer to questions, answers or allusions, the eighteen cases we present now are the only instances where the information was volunteered that the individual might be given the choice not to be reborn in the earth. For anyone who might be interested in further research, the case number (substituted in all readings for the person's name), the sex, and the age of the person at the time of the reading, is given in Appendix B. The extracts within each sub-chapter are all from the same reading unless otherwise noted. Because I quickly became bored with identifying these individuals as "this lady" or "this gentleman" and because there are so few appropriate synonyms for these vague bits of courtesy, I scratched around for some convenient substitution. Referring to them by their case numbers which were used in the transcripts seemed coldly impersonal and too reflective of the assorted series of numbers by which we all live today—from our permanently identifying Social Security number to our zip codes. I have therefore taken the liberty of assigning them pseudonyms, sometimes picked willy-nilly but often suggested by one of their past lives. No disrespect, only convenience is intended.

Each division in this chapter contains an entire reading plus an interpretation of what each portion is dealing with. In some places you may find the readings difficult to totally comprehend. With practice you can achieve a feel for the way words tumbled forth during a reading. But do get all that you can from the reading itself for much is there that is not contained in the paraphrased sections. It has been my experience over the years that different eyes and different minds will see in a reading something important another person has missed. Should I have missed some salient point, as well I might, I will appreciate hearing about it. The extracts are included for those who prefer to decide for themselves what was said.

The readings, after the suggestion had been given, first list the influencing planets, often explaining their effects. The planets, the readings stress, represent the individual's mental urges. These urges develop between earth lives in a mental plane of consciousness.

Only in the earth plane do souls have physical bodies. Life is continuous. At death these fleshly garments are laid aside, and the soul exists in another dimension, a mental plane. These interim periods, the times between lives in the earth, are referred to as planetary sojourns. This does not mean that there is life as we know it on other planets; the planets represent dimensions of consciousness. The readings say that the dimension to which the soul goes after death is determined by what the soul has done in its earth life and what the mind has dwelt upon. Learning continues even after death according to individuals' needs. When the soul again chooses to reincarnate, its mental nature and urges are the result of the interim period. The emotional nature, however, is the result of lives in the earth.

After the mental disposition of the person is given, those past lives that affect the present life are depicted. If you were to look at the transcript of the reading in the A.R.E. library, you would find that the most recent past life is presented first, and each one thereafter is further back in time. In studying these readings I found that the patterns and the progressions in a life were more easily discerned if I took them in the opposite order, working forward from the past to the present. Thus, I have rearranged the lives in chronological order.

When I started working with this material I wondered what, if anything, these individuals had in common. What can put a soul in the position in which he has a choice of returning to earth or not? And if he chooses not to return does he then return to the Source? The life readings Cayce gave show patterns of various kinds running through peoples' lives. I wondered if a common pattern could be found. Were they all saintly souls? Furthermore, had they perhaps been saintly for a series of lives? Saintliness has always seemed such a faraway goal. How important were the astrological urges? So many questions.

Gradually, as I read and reread these few choice readings, I became interested in seeing just exactly how the information was worded that caused the cases to be indexed: *Reincarnation: Unnecessary.* I found the differences in phrasing added a host of implications and further questions.

It has been said that we should learn from our successes as

15

well as from our failures, and we can most certainly learn from examples. These cases illustrate all three. For those who are tired of hearing the concept of reincarnation treated like a game of Cosmic Casting, there are some slightly different twists. Most of all they offer us hope.

A Priestess
[987]

A golden cord runs through the astrological... and the earth's experiences of this entity. The entity may complete its earth's experience in the present, if it so chooses.   987-2

What was this golden cord woven so brightly in the tapestry of this woman's experiences both in and out of the earth plane? What series of choices and purposes brought her so close to the successful completion of a cycle? The indication is clear at the outset that there is a pattern. An early suggestion is that this woman should present her knowledge of Creative Forces to others that they too might take hope.

Then, in giving that which may be helpful or beneficial to the entity in making application of those things that have and do become a part of its present experience, it is well that much that may be given be kept, be presented to others, that they, too, may take hope, may know there is *still* that hope in the *living* of those influences, those creative energies that bring into the experiences of man the knowledge of the at-oneness with that Creative Force, that Mighty I AM presence that exists, which the Giver of the good gifts has given to all.

Although the cord is said to run through planetary sojourns, meaning the time between incarnations, the reading makes clear that the woman is not at the mercy of her astrological influences; yet it states that the mental urgings prompt an entity's manifestations and choices.

We find that the astrological influences have very little to do with this entity, yet may be seen as urges in the experience and how the entity has applied those urges in the material manifestations of same.
For all in matter, all in form, first began in the urge of the mental or the spiritual influence, that *prompted* same to come into manifestations under the influence of a guiding hand.

The planets mentioned in connection with these innate

promptings are Jupiter, Venus and Uranus. The discussion of the meanings of these symbols provides hints of patterns worked out in earth lives. Because of the stress given to tolerance and faith, we also can see a definite inference that this entity's evolvement has had to do with groups of people and that her soul purpose has been much involved with teaching. We note also her interest in symbology and in mysticism.

Advice that is applicable to everyone appears throughout this reading, especially in relation to forgetting hardships and misunderstandings with other individuals as well as with groups. "Each and every soul," the reading emphasizes, "may find in a trial, in a temptation, in a hardship, even, that of beauty."

The woman was admonished to learn patience, but the stress was for her to learn patience with *herself*. The reading assured her that selfishness was not her problem, but rather the lack of patience. The paragraph that follows is an excellent example of the unique way the philosophy of the sleeping Cayce viewed seemingly familiar subjects from an unfamiliar perspective. Instead of seeing patience as passivity, the reading points out that patience is an *active* force.

In the entity we find that Jupiter is the ruling force, with Venus; which combination makes for beauty of attainment and the longing—as it is the experience of the entity—to present to others that phase, that part of the experience that is beautiful, that is better. Not to exaggeration, but rather as the entity has experienced that which is of error, that which is of shame, that which is of disrupting forces, becomes negligible unless given power by the thought, by the activity on the part of some mind. Not that denying alone makes for non-existence, but rather that those things presenting themselves as errors, as a faux pas, as a disrupting influence, may be used as the stepping-stones for the creating of those atmospheres, those environs in which each and every soul may find *in* a trial, in a temptation, in a hardship even, that of beauty. For through the things which He suffered He became the King of kings, the Lord of lords. So in man, that has named a Name that is above every name, it is found that with the using of experiences there may be brought into his consciousness that harmony, which is another name for peace, another name for good, another name for joy, which will be crowned in glory.

In the urge arising from these influences we find that there is the necessity for the entity to learn a little more of patience. For selfishness is not a portion of the entity's own being; rather is it the lack of the Patience; not with others but the more with self. For as He gave, it is in patience that ye become aware of thy soul!

So in its associations with others the entity needs to forget those things that have made for hardships, that have made for misunderstandings in relationships as one to another—whether with individuals or with groups; though the entity may find oft that it requires that self turn within, that the consciousness of His presence abiding may direct. Thus may there be brought peace and patience, as an *active* force; not as a passive influence in the experience of self but as an *active* influence!

This has brought into self that association where tolerance has not *always* been felt, as may be seen through the appearances of the entity in the earth; not tolerance as a passive thing but tolerance as an active force! For while each soul, each expression may have the right of its own opinion and its own activity, it should not only say so but act in such a manner; knowing that each soul is destined to become a portion again of the First Cause, or back to its Maker. And as there is the awareness of its individuality, its ability to apply its portion, the soul-portion of the Creative Forces or Energies or God within itself, it builds that in a *soul*-body which may be One with that Creative Force.

For while flesh and blood that is of the earth-earthy may not gain or know glory, the body—the *real* body; not the superficial but the *real* body—may become aware of its presence in the Presence of the body of God and among its brethren, and a portion of that Whole.

So does there become the awareness of tolerance in faith, that is the activity of this entity in the present, to become that which may make the ability in the entity or soul experience to use that *in hand* as the influences to know flesh save as it chooses same for its own missions for that Creative Energy.

In Jupiter we find the influences making for abilities of specific natures in the experience of the entity; as in constructive thinking for individuals and for groups, whether this be for writing or for instruction in this or that form. It will find in the application of self there may be much given to others, in the form of papers, in the forms of charts, in the form of instruction that may become—as it were—a light set on a hill for many who grope in darkness and in doubt, who are fearful. For that quieting through the gaining of patience in self may enable the entity to give that light and that instruction necessary for the guiding of many.

Venus makes for close friendships with those whom the entity finds in its experience; not only as a great love for its fellow man but in making for ties that hold, of the spirit rather than of the flesh. Hence kindred souls in all walks of life may find in associations with the entity much that becomes as a complement, as a helpmate to their own struggles. This is expressed in a truth He gave: "Who is my brother? Who is my mother? Who is my sister? They that do the will of my father in heaven, the same are my mother, my brother, my sister."

This is the love that all should come to know, even as it has been attained in a great measure by this entity through the experiences it has gained in its sojourns. And more and more will the entity become aware of same in *active* tolerance and *active* patience.

In Uranus we find the extremist influences, that have been experienced by the entity in the present and that come as urges in the experiences day by day. Oft, from that sojourn or environ in the Uranian experience, does the entity find itself *impelled*—as it were—to do this or that which may be entirely at variance to what reason or cold reason would tell the entity. And it makes for those experiences with its friendships, or a certain portion of same, wherein the entity seems to be—or appears to others to be—*somewhat* peculiar or odd in its choice of this or that activity in relationships to its associations, its readings, its study, its line of endeavor in this or that manner of recreation.

All of these become a portion of the entity's urge and experience; as does also the interest in things that are psychic or occult or mystic, these have a part in the urges in the experience of the entity. Hence mystical signs, mystical numbers, mystical conditions have much to do with the entity at times. And these may come in the *vision* and in the dreams (that have been for the time set aside), more and more as the entity turns to those patience applications.

For, as will be seen, the entity made *for* the Priest the Urim and the Thummim! [Exodus 28:30]

And the entity may give much of that which comes as an influence in the experiences through the deeper meditation; much constructive counsel to those that seek into the mysteries that are hidden in the activities of those who would give their expression of that they have conceived from the Spirit, that *motivates* them in their activities.

Then, in these do we find the greater influences from the astrological sojourns.

The continuing effect of astrological urges is evidenced in the answer to a question this woman submitted to Cayce.

Q-1. Have I an inferiority complex, and what can I do to overcome it?
A-1. As we have indicated, through the urge from the Uranian influence we find experiences that make for individuals speaking so as to make the entity conscious that it has acted quickly without thought; that it has acted quickly by an urge from within; but not an inferiority complex. Rather is there the necessity, as we have indicated, to meet such experiences with patience, and to have *tolerance* with those that misjudge. For say oft, "They know not what they do!"

Tracing patterns that developed and recurred through various lives in the earth is most easily done when one starts with the earliest life mentioned in a Cayce reading. That is to say, one would start at the end of the reading because, when Cayce reviewed past lives, he began with the most recent life and concluded with the earliest life that was affecting the individual.

Egypt, India and Mongolia

Of the four lives said to be influencing the current life, the earliest was in Egypt when people gathered from all over the earth to correlate the truth. This woman was a native Egyptian who had been cleansed in the Temple of Sacrifice and had gone on to service in the Temple Beautiful. After a period of counseling and teaching, she became the first representative of the Temple Beautiful in India. Later she had gone on to the Gobi land (Mongolia) where she became a priestess in the Temple of Gold (which the reading says is still intact there). The great development in that life accounted for her present abilities in teaching, ministering and leading.

. . . the entity was in the land now known as the Indian and Egyptian, during those periods when there were the gatherings of those from many of the lands for the correlating of the truths that were presented by Saneid in the Indian land, by Ra Ta in the Egyptian land, by Ajax from the Atlantean land, by those from the Carpathian land, by those from the Pyrenees, by those from the Incal and those from the Oz lands, and by those from that activity which will again be uncovered in the Gobi land.

And *here* the entity may find a great interest, a great power, in the instructions and help that it may lend to others in their choosing the places of seeking for that knowledge that may make for a more universality of thought *throughout* the universe in spiritual lines.

Then the entity was among the natives of the Egyptian land, and rose to power through those cleansings in the Temple of Sacrifice; then becoming a portion of the activative service in the Temple Beautiful when it made for those abilities within self to mete out to many those things necessary in their physical and mental understanding.

And with the correlating of the thought, the entity became first as the representative of the Temple Beautiful in the Indian land; and later—and during the period of its greatest height—in the land of the Gobi, or the Mongoloid. *There* the entity was as the Priestess in the Temple of Gold, which is still intact there.

The entity then, as Shu-Shent, made for great development; and from those experiences in the present comes the abilities for the teachings, for the ministerings, for the leading of many.

When she incarnated again, she was a daughter of Levi and among the chosen people in the wilderness. This was during a period when the chosen people were being given the manner in which they should worship in the temple. Thus she carries into her present life a deep-seated interest in temple worship.

The Cayce readings say no ability or training is lost from one life to the next. This life shows her to have counseling ability and to be familiar with the mysteries and underlying meanings of symbology. There appears, however, a mention of *fear*. In this instance it was the fear that a group of people could, through misunderstanding, misdirection, or misplacement of values, be led astray.

Before that we find the entity was in that land, that period, when the chosen people were being given upon the holy mount the manner of their exercise in the temple, or in the service before the tabernacle.

The entity then was among the daughters of Levi, and those chosen to make the vestment of the priest. And to the entity, because of its own abilities, there was given the preparation of the settings of the breastplate and the putting of the stones thereon, and the preparation of the Urim and Thummim for the interpretations of the movements that came upon the high priest in the holy of holies to be given to his people in or from the door of the tabernacle.

Then in the name Henriettah, the entity's activities were in a high force *equal to* the cousin, Miriam.

Throughout the experience the entity gained; for it reasoned with Nadab and Abihu; it counseled for Korah, yet did not allow self to become entangled in any of those influences that would have made for the rise to the position of fame. Rather did the entity choose to remain as one in the background that there might be given the greater understanding to that mighty people as they stood in the presence of the I AM that had brought them to the holy mount.

In the present from that sojourn, those things pertaining to the mysteries of the temple, the mysteries of numbers, of figures, and those things that have their hidden meaning, become as a portion of the entity. Yet oft does there arise that sudden change as to the fearfulness of people giving too great a power to such things that would lead them astray; as they did in the experience of the entity in the wilderness.

Persia

While among the children of Israel, the entity had not allowed herself to become entangled in striving for fame and power, yet both fame and power were forthcoming in the next life. Once again appearing in a period when a great teacher was promulgating Truth to a people, she seems to have had a life filled with healing and harmony. The reading traces her love of oriental things to that period and indicates that Eastern music and chanting would awaken her memory of the life in Persia.

Before that we find the entity was in the land now known as the Persian or Abrabian, when there were the gatherings of many to the city in the hills and in the plains.

The entity was of those Persian peoples, or the first of the Croesus'; being in the relations to or in the household of the king.

And as there came to be the greater understanding of the tenets and truths given by the teacher Uhjltd, that brought not only health in the body but a balance in the mental minds of those that came to the city in the plains for instructive forces, the entity was one who rose to the position of the Princess after the destruction of the king's daughter in the raid.

Then the entity rose to power, through the healing that was brought in the body from the leader in the tented city.

And as it made application of those tenets, as it gathered those of its own household and of its own kingdom for the profession and application of those things that had been gathered from the teacher, much came to the entity and to the surroundings of same, in power, in glory, in the beautiful things that were builded in that land.

From that experience in the present the entity finds that those things oriental, those things pertaining to the Persian plaids and Persian silks, those brocaded conditions that were made by many of the entity's associates for their helpfulness in bringing beauty to those peoples, become—as it were—an influence in the entity's present experience.

And those tenets held as we have indicated will make for harmonious experience and the joy of same; as do certain sounds of music, certain sounds of chant, certain sounds of activity, bring to the entity an awakening and a consciousness of movement from within that awakens something as the entity experienced during that sojourn.

New England

Many lives in temple service—as missionary, priestess, princess, counselor, teacher—had prepared her for the one as Nancy Connelly, the minister's wife. The experience was in Salem, Massachusetts, at the time of the witch hunts. Many of her present family, and much of her current life, were profoundly influenced by that era. There is continuing interest in and sympathy with the occult. She was said to have gained in mental and spiritual experience. But the emotional flavor of the time, acting in conjunction with the long implanted fear of the dreadful power of a group, left its mark upon her. A fear of physical suffering, as well as fear of criticism was due to that life. It was toward this area of attitude, then, that the reading enjoined her to learn to be tolerant, to forget hardships and misunderstandings, and most of all, to learn to be patient with herself.

As to the appearances in the earth and those that influence the entity in the present, we find—while far apart in their activity—these have been those that bring to the entity much of the urges that arise through the emotional nature of the entity in *this present* manifestation, or materialization:

Before this we find the entity was in the land of the present nativity, but in and about that known as the Vinland—or about Provincetown and Salem, during the early periods of those activities when the persecutions arose for those who heard the unusual, who experienced the moving of an influence or force from without themselves.

The *entity* then was close to many of those who were beset by such experiences; hearing, knowing, experiencing many sides of the material manifestations; hearing and knowing many sides of the influences in the experiences of those that *had* the meetings and were acquainted with such activities.

Then the entity was close to, and the companion of, the minister in the Salem activity; one Nancy Donnelly.

In the experience the entity gained; yet those things that made for the fear of material suffering, the fear of what people said in criticism, builded much that was hard to be borne in the experience of the entity during that sojourn. Yet the entity, it may be said, gained in the mental and spiritual experience; and has brought to this present sojourn that influence wherein the entity hears much that others would say or would give of their activity, of their experience, and has judged oft well, has judged oft according to those experiences as the minister's helper.

This is a portion that must be met in that activity of tolerance, in that active patience in self.

The abilities from that sojourn are towards the setting down of data pertaining to the intricate activities or details of an experience; these become a portion of the entity in its greater activity.

The entity's social life, its marital life, its relations with its blood *in* the present have arisen much from those experiences.

The weirdness of Salem, also the weirdness of the vault or any of those places wherein the dead have buried their dead, finds a gloom within the entity's experience. Yet those places of beauty where there is honor for memory, the trust is in the living God, bring an uplifting in the inmost being of the entity. These are from those experiences, as it heard the sound of those calls during that Provincetown period.

The golden cord. What was it? It might be the dedication to an ideal that appeared consistently in each earthly expression. It might be the thread of service that is evident in each. That teaching was a definite soul purpose is obvious from the outset. Perhaps the golden cord was her innate faith in the oneness of truth, for at the end of her reading, the woman was told:

Keep that faith thou *innately* hast in the oneness of power in the Creative Forces as it makes for manifestations in the hearts and minds of men; and as ye do it in thy activities with thy fellow man, as ye do it in thy meditation, as ye do it in thy mind, so will it be meted to thee in thine inner self. For all must pass under the *rod;* but He has tempered this with mercy and judgment. So must ye temper thine judgments, so must ye find thy patience, so must ye find those things within self that make for the answer of thyself before the Throne of grace. For if ye would have mercy ye must show mercy to thy fellow man; yea to thine very enemy, to those that despitefully use you. Laugh with those who laugh; mourn with those who mourn, in the Lord. *Keep* thy paths straight, and ye will find *glory*—glory—unto thyself!
In the writing of books, in the ministry of tracts or tenets that may be helpful in song, in verse, in these are thy activities. But forsake not thy faith in the *oneness* of Truth!   987-2

The choice of returning to earth again was said to be *hers.*

A Favorite
[569]

One that is in the influence of love's forces ever.
569-6

We'll call her Ella, this hardworking spinster. The brief facts about her twentieth-century incarnation are bleak. She kept house for her widowed stepmother and helped bring up two younger half-brothers. Throughout her adult life she remained single in deference to her stepmother's wishes. In one letter Ella wrote that she considered this earthly life, "a vale of tears." Much encouragement came from her life reading. There is a strong inference that the present karmic situation held the possibility for great spiritual advancement.

The Influencing Planets

In taking the position in the present earth's plane, we find [the entity] under the influence of Jupiter and Venus, with

Mercury and Uranus in the distance. In the adverse influence then of Vulcan and of the Pleiades. Hence the conditions as have to do with the relations in the present earth's sphere.

As to the personality as is exhibited in the present earth plane, we find one ever given to those ennobling influences in Jupiter and Venus. Then with love, with prudence, with truth, with all of these classifications of those virtues as are found in the relation of Venus and Jupiter. See, there's a whole lot of money due the body that it has never gotten, and with the influences then in the life, there is brought these conditions as the latent forces in the urges of entity:

One that is considered peculiar by many, in its action, in its thought. One that is in the influence of love's forces ever. One that is lover of nature, of developing nature in every way, in the beauties in nature, in flowers, in music, in art, in every nature of the studies and the spirit as is manifest in same, and we shall see from the position many of these urges are taken.

One that may give much joy to many peoples, always giving, giving, more than ever receiving.

Egypt

The three lives mentioned as affecting Ella have several ideas in common. In each she was a favorite of a prominent person, and each experience was during a time of division. What is not immediately evident is that in each incarnation she was closely associated with her step-cousin (Case 538) with whom she had been brought up. In the Egyptian incarnation she had replaced that lady as the king's favorite.

. . . we find in the Egyptian forces, when the division in the kingdom came, on account of the rule of the Priesthood [time of Ra Ta]. The entity then in the household of that ruler, and was a favorite with the then ruler, and siding with the ruler [341] and becoming the chief in that court after the banishment of [the] Priest and those associated, or followers of same. [G.D.'s note: She replaced 538 as king's favorite when 538 was banished with Ra Ta.] Then first in the name is Isisush. Changed, when the coming of high estate in the rule, to Ahahs, and the entity both developed and retarded in that rule, gaining much of those innate desires toward that of close work with the needle, or with the hand, in any fancy work, for many of the alba garments were then first given shape by those hands, and many may yet be found in those tombs as exist to this day.

Persia and Greece

Captured and removed from her native Persia, she benefited. From this life Ella gained her inner security, a determination to stick to her purposes, and an innate satisfaction in the knowledge she gained at that time.

In the one before this we find in the Persian rule, when the forces were being overrun by the Grecians, and the entity then [was] carried as one of the captives to that country [period of Uhjltd] being then in the name Aurial, and in the household of the friend to the one who afterward gave much of the first philosophy of faith to this people, yet being persecuted for that belief and action. In this we find the entity as Aurial developed much and gained much in the knowledge of the mental developments as were seen in the human forces. The urges as we see in the present from this, when once set in mind as to purpose or intent, hard to change, for that innate feeling of self's satisfaction in the gained knowledge, as acquired through that sojourn, ever projects itself in the inner consciousness.

France and England

In the household of those who sheltered Charles II, she was a favorite of that ruler. Her fastidiousness in dress, and her ability to keep secrets were credited to that life.

In the one before this we find in France, in the days when the Second Charles was in exile. The entity then in the name of Asada, and in the household of those who sheltered the escaped man or ruler afterwards, and assisted in the keeping of soldiery from capturing same, and was ever a favorite of that ruler, and the latter days were spent in the foreign port from birth, in England, see? and the urges as seen, the particular care in dress, and ability to keep secrets more than ordinary.

The reading ended with this inspiring promise:

... keep in that same way as has been set in self, in purpose and in manner, for through the own efforts in self there need not be the necessity in returning to earth's plane, for as is set, and if kept, these would develop into the higher spiritual realms, and then keep self in that way that leads to life everlasting, for in Him whom thou hast put thy trust is Life, for He is the Way, the Truth, the Light. In Him there is no guile. We are through for the present.   569-6

The clue as to the reason this possibility might be open to her is not delineated in the lives mentioned. Most probably the hint is within the discussion of the astrological aspects, where Ella is said to be "in the influence of love's forces, ever," and "always giving, giving, more than receiving."

A Peacemaker
[1143]

The desire for help to those that are weary of their
mental and material burdens ... finds an answering
within the inmost being of the entity.   1143-2

This case has several points in common with others who were
told that the present incarnation might be the last in the earth
plane. First, her planets include Jupiter and Venus. Second,
there is a pattern of incarnating during times of turmoil and
gaining as a result. Third, the entity is said to have "Given,
given, given of self." Yet certainly, spiritual perfection has not
been reached, for the reading points out that she must be
careful not to feel sorry for herself.

When he started to give the information on past lives, Mr.
Cayce in this reading went back audibly over the years to the
birth date, commenting periodically on periods of change. Then
he seemed to see the influences surrounding her birth. He said
that although the entity's lives had been during periods of great
strife, she had managed to keep a balance within and had
learned tolerance.

Antagonism and destruction often existed in the world
around her. And at times additional anxieties arose due to her
astrological aspects. Yet all of these experiences had helped her
to develop patience.

As to the experiences then of this entity, [1143] called in the
present (What a beautiful surrounding in its entrance into this
earth in the present!), we find in the astrological aspects much
has been gained and maintained by the entity that would be
well for others to make a part of themselves in their own
application.

For while throughout the experiences and sojourns in the
earth turmoils of many natures have arisen, especially upon
large scales of antagonistic influence, troublesome periods by
animosities and waywardnesses upon the part of individuals
and groups and masses about the entity, with these the entity
has kept an equal balance, especially in what may be termed in
words as tolerance.

Not that there have not been anxieties even in its spiritual or
astrological aspects, yet these as an innate and as a manifested
experience become a portion of the entity itself.

And—as is the fruit of same—patience as engendered by
mercy, has accompanied these experiences.

In introducing the affecting planets, the reading indicates
that Jupiter brings an ability to be helpful to those who are

working in harmony with Creative Forces. It stresses her great reliability in positions of trust.

Thus the phases of the entity's sojourns then in the environs called astrological become apparent as with new meanings to some from those environments.

Jupiter—we find the association as towards a *helpfulness* in the engendering associations with those in power, those in positions of prominence as to their engendering for others conditions that make for the developments toward brotherly love in their brotherly love in their activity.

These then make from the material aspect for that upon which the entity is active, finding in its associations great abilities, those that have been entrusted with means, manners and ways of dealing with their fellow man.

And the entity has been, and will ever be so long as these are held, inviolate as a tempering experience for all such.

To Venus is ascribed the fact that the entity was always surrounded with the influences of beauty and peace. This was the result of action, not idleness; she had gained tranquility not by sitting quietly, but by bringing peace into the lives of others.

Also in those influences from Venus we find that beauty, peace, harmonious forces are ever in and *about* the entity; yet for such to become active in the experience there has been required upon the part of the entity an *activity*. Not placidness, but peace rather gained, rather felt, rather experienced by *bringing* same into the experience of others.

Even benevolent is the influence of Uranus which signifies the extremes in personality. In this instance, combined with the soul's tolerance and patience, it enabled the individual to empathize with and help others.

We find also in those astrological sojourns or influences in Uranus making for extremes; that the entity through its earthly as well as through the innate forces that have been impelled or chosen by self has found itself swinging, as it were, oft *suddenly* from extreme to extreme.

Yet in its ability from a soul force, that finds expressions in those words we term as tolerance, patience, the entity has found the abilities to aid here and there.

The appearance of Mars occasioned the warnings not to feel sorry for herself, and not to fall prey to self-exaltation. It was stated that she could continue to be a harmonious influence if she avoids these two possibilities.

28

Hold fast to these. For while those influences from Martian experiences make for turmoils as about, we find that—unless it allows itself to become, as it were, at times sorry for itself, or to become in a manner affected through such experiences that arise for self-aggrandizement—the entity may continue then to bring harmonious influences in the experiences of those whom the entity may contact in the materiality.

The reading goes on to assert that, because the various astrological influences have been manifested so well in the physical plane, it is difficult to interpret whether the operative urges are the effect of lives in the earth, or the time between lives. In this segment of the reading, the lady is told of the possibility that she may not need to incarnate again in the earth.

These influences, of course, as indicated, arise innately; yet *so well,* so oft have these been manifested in the physical and material application of the entity. To differentiate becomes rather hard in making for an interpretation of that which has been recorded here.
This entity may, with the keeping of those developments, make its peace in such a manner as for there to be few or none of the turmoils of the earth in its experience again.
As to the influences from the sojourns in the earth, while these are not *all,* they are those that in the present make for the urges that the entity finds indicated in its experiences and in its meeting with its fellow man in their problems, in their turmoils.
For, as the entity has in the most of its sojourns from the earth GIVEN—GIVEN—GIVEN of self, so has there come in the deeper recesses of the present experiences—even upon the heels of turmoils, even upon the mount of consternation—a deeper and an abiding peace that comes only with that as He hath given, "MY PEACE I LEAVE WITH YOU." Not as the world knoweth or giveth peace, but that which makes for those answers as from within, when there is the turning to that Great Giver of love, mercy, justice—"Well done, thou good and faithful servant." For ye shall indeed know the joys of thy Lord. Hold fast, stand steadfast with the armor of thy Lord near thee.

Egypt

As a follower of the Priest Ra Ta during a disruptive period of prehistory, the entity gained much. She specifically learned that to strike back when attacked only multiplies strife and makes it harder to set one's own life in order.

Before that we find the entity was in the land now known as

the Egyptian, during those periods when there were turmoils and strifes to those peoples that had settled in the land, and attempted to build for those peoples roundabout an understanding of the relationships of man to the Creative Forces, of man to his own fellow man.

The entity was among those peoples joined nigh to that one made the Priest, and who was debarred or set adrift from the activities begun.

Those periods and experiences brought turmoils to the entity, yet with the return of the Priest, with the activities of those that came from Atlantis, with the paralleling of the teachings by the emissaries from Saneid, from On [?], from the activities in the Gobi, the entity began then to know that he that smiteth thee, if thou dost smite in return, will but engender an animosity that grows, that becomes as briers and tares in thine own experience, that will hinder thee in thine *own* activity, bringing disturbing forces that make for the engendering of hate.

The name then was Absi-Shupht, and much might be said as to that development there.

The Holy Land

The life in Egypt had started a cycle of interest in temple worship. At that time, the Priest was attempting to build an understanding of the relationship of man to the Creative Forces and of man's relationship to man. When this entity appeared in the Holy Land among the chosen people, it was at a time when the tabernacle was being reestablished. It was a time of turmoil, also, as the children of Israel entered the Promised Land. Now named Belenda she was helpful in acting as a nurse, and in bringing understanding of the king's edict to his people. Losses during the experience resulted when Belenda resented not being understood. Her motives were doubted. Once again she is warned to be tolerant, "even with those that despitefully use thee."

Before that we find the entity was in those periods when there was the return of a chosen people to their land for the reestablishing in the land of promise of a ritual service.

There the entity, with Zerubbabel's handmaids, became a helpful influence. And with the coming then of the priest—or princess—and the prince in Nehemiah, we find the entity lent that aid which made for the helping of those that resisted the peoples roundabout. Not by might, not by power, but by lending a helping hand to those that suffered bodily; aiding in bringing to those a better understanding of that edict which was given by the king for the reestablishing of those services of a people in their *own* land.

Then the name was Belenda, and the entity gained, lost, gained through the experience. For being misjudged for the associations with those then as of the heathens roundabout, as termed by those strangers in their own home land, the entity felt within self as being misunderstood—and condemned, when innately within self there was known how the protection was brought even to many of those that labored upon the wall, as well as in those that were established.

Yet if the entity will read very closely the 6th and 8th chapters of Nehemiah, it will find much that harkens for an awareness of its presence there.

Hold to those things that make for this ability to be tolerant, even with those that despitefully use thee. For it engenders strife to hold animosities.

England

Another rough period in history was the setting for Belenda's next life. Her name was Marjorie and she lived in England during the time when the Norsemen, the Huns and the Gauls were taking turns ravaging the country. It was a time of fear and violence when even neighbors could not be trusted. Yet this life in Lancastershire (now called Lancashire) presented the girl with the opportunity to keep a balance within herself, and to aid others in doing the same. She was told that the Lancastershire area even in the present would bring feelings of sorrow, but also a deep gladness. The fact that this deep gladness is within her makes it possible to bring harmony to those around her.

Before this we find the entity lived in the earth during those periods when there was the overrunning, or when the changes were coming about in the land of nativity, when there were the Norsemen with the Huns and the Gauls that made for the turmoils in the north and in the eastern portion of the land.

The entity was then in the name (hence it is well named in the present) Marjorie.

In the experience there were those turmoils and strifes, with neighbor against neighbor oft; for it was during those periods when they each of the landholders or of the different groups were as a law in their own land.

The entity kept a balance between many of those in and about the land, in Lancastershire, where there is to the entity—in those surroundings in the present—much that makes for deep meditation; for sorrow, yet punctured much and oft with a deeper gladness for the experiences that come there.

And as the entity was in those fields and among those blossoms when they began to fade, it finds those sadnesses that yet bring a joy and a comfort in the inner self.

31

Hence in the introspection of self gladness is ever present, yet it is tinged with the desire for help to those that are weary of their mental and material burdens—that finds an answering within the inmost being of the entity itself.

For as the entity gained in those experiences, so may it in the present find that—not by might or power, as saith the Lord of hosts, but by the still small voice, by the counsel as of one tempered with mercy, grace and peace—it may bring to those whom the entity contacts in such disturbing forces the experiences of *harmony* within self.

Coming back to the present, the reading points to specific Biblical passages containing the precepts which she has taken as her creed.

As to the abilities in the present, and that to which the entity may attain, and how:

Who would dare give the entity counsel when it may counsel so well! Hold fast to that which has been or may be gained by the reading of the 30th chapter of Deuteronomy, the 14th of Joshua, the 24th Psalm, the 12th of Romans; the 14th, 15th, 16th, 17th as recorded to John. For there ye will see that thou has *innately* made as thy bond. For He *is* in His holy temple and would speak with thee; for *thy* body, *too,* is His temple, and there He meets with thee!

Love the Lord, eschew evil, keep the faith. For it *is* but a reasonable service.   1143-2

A sense of duty often has carried this Peacemaker into the center of strife and empowered her to introduce—by means of simple acts, a sense of stability.

A Glad Helper
[560]

Keep that committed, for those that seek through
love will find.   560-1

Martha in the Bible has become almost synonymous with the no-nonsense, practical approach to life. This individual was told by her reading that she, indeed, had been that Martha. The astrological aspects given in the beginning of the reading evoke a picture of another no-nonsense, practical lady. At the time her reading was given, Martha was forty-five, unmarried and lived with a younger sister (993) who also had had readings. That they had been sisters three times previously suggests strong karmic ties.

32

The astrological aspects describe Martha as being considered high-minded and with a tendency to be dictatorial in manner—a characteristic not infrequently associated with older sisters. However, the reading acknowledges that she, unlike many others, has been working on this.

In entering, we find in astrological aspects many *varying* conditions; while Pisces, just past, in the rising of influences from this—with the Mercurian, Venus, Jupiter and Uranus, these bring in an *astrological* manner many *varying* aspects of experiences in the influence, or the entity influenced in many varying manners as to that as is builded, or has been builded in the present experience of the entity, has depended upon the manner in which the entity itself has applied its will as respecting same. These, as we find, are builded in the entity *for* experiences, *irrespective* of how will's influence *has* been applied. *These,* as we find, have been builded as *how* the entity *has* applied will as respecting same:
In those influences in Mercury—oft has the entity been considered not only high-minded, but tendency towards the dictatorial in mien and manner, though the application of *will* in *respect* to such has altered this in a great degree as to the *influences* impelled by the positiveness *of* the entity in its application toward such influences. *Well* (this aside, please) were the fact, as has been builded by the entity, that many would do likewise.

Martha sounds as if she might have been the undemonstrative type. The reading states that she is loved by all who really get to know her; yet, because of her personality, people are not necessarily inclined to express their fondness for her. It points out that she treasures her friendships and remains steadfast in them. It says that although she doesn't hold grudges, she doesn't easily forget slights. Nevertheless, she's been conscious of this as an attitude to overcome. Her spiritual life has developed to such an extent that, should she keep in her present attunement, she need not return again to the earth.

In the influences in Venus makes for that of one that is loved by all who come to know the entity *as* a whole, yet the application of self respecting same has not *drawn* all to express themselves in a manner as would signify that [in] their feelings toward the entity. Not that the entity had, or has, held self *aloof* from peoples, but rather that, those that have *known* the entity best have learned to love the entity the more. In this application, this has drawn *to* the entity, *for* the entity, friendships that once made *seldom* have they been broken, save by those who have so acted, so acted in their *own* feelings, as to separate themselves from that influence. This has the tendency at times (as the entity has changed much) for the grudges, or the holding of activities of others in a manner—not as grudge, but a tendency to not easily forget slights or differences; yet in the *building* much has been lost in the bigness of the influences gained in Jupiter *and* Uranus in this respect, for the *spiritual* life *of* the entity is such to have *builded* for a development in this present plane to such an extent—that is, the *desire* such, and kept in the present attunement—the earth need hold no cares for the entity in or after this experience.

The broadness of vision attributed to Jupiter enables Martha to see beyond the obvious and the ordinary. The last sentence in this segment predicts that she will be able to be a spiritual leader and doing so will bring her great development. She did in fact become the leader of the Glad Helpers Prayer Group and acted in this capacity for seven years, until her death in 1939.

In Jupiter we find one that has broad vision of any subject, no matter how very centralized a portion of the subject or matter is taken by the entity, no matter how definite the aims of the entity towards conditions, peoples, places or *philosophies*—even—the *vision* is that that *enables* the entity to reach far beyond that as is ordinarily understood. With the ascendancy of this influence, after the fifteenth of the coming month, for years there will *still* be the tendency for an expansion of influences in these directions, of enabling others to so centralize their efforts and their visions as to gain a better concept of that portion of life's experience they, or individuals, are seeking. Hence, as one that would direct in the centralizing of individuals' desires for the seeking of spiritual guidance, mental understanding, material aid in a physical sphere, will *be* the work, the greater developing period of, and *abilities* of the entity in this present experience.

The influence of Uranus is said to be responsible for what appears to be indifference in her manner. One gets the picture of a lady trying out of politeness not to be curious, and thus giving observers the impression of total disinterest in them and their problems. The reading says that she could often be of help, if asked. This evidently was a concern to her, but the reading states that the rising influence of Jupiter would in the coming years bring a fuller understanding.

In those influences in Uranian, makes for those little appearances of indifference in the entity's mien, when it has as much curiosity as any! yet the appearance and acts may be as not the interest, but desiring not to show to be curious, or to delve into other people's affairs or business! yet the influences as are seen, that oft the entity—in its *intuitive* natures—if asked, could often help when others *feel* indifference has kept them from seeking when they would desire to. This, in the application, the entity has kept rather as a sacred portion of its own experience. At times it has brought those qualms of conscience that has made for wonderments as to whether it has appeared too indifferent or not, or as to whether there has been as much interest shown as self *should* have manifested or expressed; yet with the opportunities as may be opened through those experiences with the rising influence in Jupiter—which will bring, with the square of Venus in the love's influence, as is seen, many experiences that will make for a larger, fuller, greater understanding to the entity in these coming years, and months, and days.

Egypt

The earliest life given shows Martha in Egypt closely associated with the Priest and active in the temple service. She is said to have gained through the experience, losing only when she was sent abroad and got side-tracked by fun and games. Even the losing, the reading points out, is part of her development because it enables her to understand other seekers and their motives. Her practical nature is noted and that she could help others find the best avenues for their development.

In the one then before this we find in that land now known as the Egyptian, and during that period when there were rebellions in the land, and when there had been the reestablishing of those that were deposed. The entity came into the *temple* service there, being *then* closely associated with the Priest as was deposed [Ra Ta], and became close to those that were of the temple service, gaining in the experience, losing only when the secular things of the world when the entity sent abroad with others—made forgetfulness come in the experiences of the entity in that period. In the name Isusi. In the present, this experience has—as of those in desert and in the Holy City—brought much of that, with the Uranian influence, that makes for abilities to aid in an understanding of that as *is* the *desire* of those that would seek. Being practical, there makes for those abilities—as to whether that sought is of the *material* sources, the spiritual foundations, or of a mental aptitude towards the attempts to cover up or hide the real purpose. In this field, then, may the entity gain the most in the present, in aiding those who would seek to find—in the various forces as they manifest in the entity's experiences—*that* which *that* individual seeks. That is, as the entity—through its breadth of experience and understanding—may aid another in knowing what phase *of* the forces *manifested,* an individual may find *their* greater blessing.

Persia

Closely associated with the priest Ra Ta in Egypt, she appeared later in Persia associated closely with Uhjltd. Both Ra Ta and Uhjltd were incarnations of Edgar Cayce. Both periods were said to be eras in which the same work was going on as is being put forth today by the philosophy in the Cayce readings. Thus we see Martha had strong early ties to the work of the A.R.E. The experience in Persia helped Martha improve her general attitude. Nevertheless, her quickness to feel slighted is mentioned again.

In the one then before this we find in that land when there were those comings together in the land now known as the Persian or Arabian land, when Uhjltd gathered many peoples about those cities being builded. The entity among those that came in, and were of those that—in the *household* of the leader—came in contact with, associated *with,* many of those of the household. In this association the entity changed much in its attitude towards people, things, conditions and surroundings. Hence in this experience may be termed the change in the entity's activities, as is seen what was brought in the one that followed. In this experience may be seen that as has been builded, or as has been overcome, of the little grudges, or the little feelings oft of slight or of oppressions, "I will get even at some time—not *mine,* but it will be done!" This may be overcome, *has* been overcome much, may it be taken away—even as has been given. In this experience in the name Raoue.

The Promised Land

The life as Martha, sister of Lazarus whom Jesus raised from the dead, was very important in her current life. The name was given in the question period. The high ideals from her lives in Egypt and Persia, were applied in her daily life in Bethany. This section places great emphasis on her practical nature and her belief that everyone must do his best in whatever situation he finds himself. She was a dreamer, but one with a realistic approach to life.

In the one before this we find in that land now known as the promised land, and during that period when there were the walkings in the land of the Promised One. The entity among those that were close *to* the Master, being then the sister to one of those that the Master raised from the dead [Lazarus], living in Bethany in that experience. Hence those of that period are near and dear, and far *from* those things that hinder from *knowing* of those that would separate the entity from those experiences! Gaining, sure, through the experience, and giving much to many; though called by those that in the experience would bring censure for the parts chosen [as Martha], or those of the secular things of life, yet in the present—with the experience—brings that *practicability* of the entity, that in groups, in associations, has ever been called—while the dreamer, yet all practical thought must be in accord *with* the life lived, with the circumstances as surround, with the conditions in which people find themselves—*these* are the better part, as was in that experience.

England

The next life affecting Martha was in England in the household of Charles I. The reading said that she gained because she was able to aid the suffering members of that household. Here is the practical Martha again, doing what she sees to do wherever she is, relieving fear, teaching, offering spiritual guidance. She also helped in material ways—when necessary, acting as a spy. The life in England enabled her to broaden her insight and heightened her Martha characteristic of not wasting time talking when things needed to be done.

In the one then before this we find in that land [England] of nativity (that is, of the present), during those periods when there were those rebellions *through* the land, and the entity of those in the household of him, the ruler, that was beheaded [Charles I]. The entity then gained through the oppressions in that land, being able then to aid those that were *of* that house, even she [Queen Henrietta] that suffered by the acts of those that took the life *of* the ruler. The entity aided in making for the quietings of the fears, through those teachings of the faith that makes one strong, even under physical oppression. Being also among those that give aid to the young king [Charles II] in his escape to the foreign land, aiding also with those that cared for this ruler in the foreign land, becoming an emissary—or what would be called in the present a political spy, the entity was able to give much aid in *material* ways, and with the spiritual guidance as held, much of a mental and *spiritual* aid to those contacted. In the name Erial. In the present experience, while those experiences of the period bring many of those little hesitancies as come from speaking when there is the thought of things to be done or accomplished, yet gives to the entity the insight of a broad field of experience.

Virginia

The last and most recent life was in Virginia. During the question period she asked to be given her name from that time and was told it had been Geraldine Fairfax and that records could be found in the area around Fredericksburg, Virginia. We have no information on whether she ever tried to find them. The reading suggests that she might suffer claustrophobia. Later, when her sister had a reading (993-4) she asked for more specifics about that and was told that Geraldine Fairfax, just entering her teens, had lost her life being crushed in the earth in a cave-in around some new construction.

One section traces to this life a dislike of people taking too much pride in their lineage. Practical Martha feels, of course, that what is more important is what one does for others, not what someone in the past has done for them. There is no hint here as to just who oppressed her, or how, yet we are told that she gained because of the love she had for them.

In the one then just before this we find in the land chosen *now* as the dwelling land [Virginia], and among those peoples as settled in the new land. The entity's experiences were of those that were *leading* as frontiersmen, yet in a period when those of the earth had brought forth those of bounty to the people, yet during the period of oppression, and during those periods as brought on by the aggressiveness of those sires in the period of the entity in the Fairfax land. The entity lost through those oppressions, and losing the life early in the experience by being crushed in earth; and masses brings that *physical* innate influence of crowds, or *smothering feelings* close to the entity, as if it must *soon* be free! In this experience the entity finds that while there are *many* who boast of their lineage, or of their relations, rather does *self* find that, that *builded* as to aiding another speaks much more than that as of *others'* accomplishments for them. *Proud* indeed of the associations and relations, as all *should* be—for to have *chosen* a way that brings its reward in the *material* way may one be proud, yet not haughty *with* same. In this experience gaining and losing. Losing under the expressions of those that would oppress, yet *gaining* in the love held even for those that oppressed.

These lives show an almost unbroken commitment to the highest ideals and to the practical application of them. The reading ends with this admonition:

In the present, then, keep—as was in old—those experiences that make for the *understanding* of those forces *in* love as were manifested in the home in Bethany. Keep that committed, for those that seek *through* love will find. Those that seek through any *other* source may be dumbfounded in the maze of that as is presented.   560-1

A tireless worker, Martha has served well. She seems to have just about fulfilled the duties set for her here.

A Counselor
[2903]

One that gives to the development of others in
every plane.   2903-1

This man was a special representative for a life insurance company at the time he requested his reading, but the reading emphatically states that he would have made a wonderful minister.

Starting as usual with the astrological urges, the reading points to the ennobling influences from Jupiter and Mercury, and states that the entity inspired faith in others and radiated unselfishness. Noting the presence of Mars among the significant planets, the reading comments on his strong temper. This he was not only able to control but also was able to channel beneficially. In fact, all adverse influences were used for development.

Within the section of the reading describing the mental urges was the comment that the man could, " ... with the present will forces, make self unnecessary for return in the earth's spheres."

As to the present position, we find taken from that of Jupiter, with Mercury and Mars in both adverse and in good influences in the present earth's plane. Then, we find one with those high ennobling influences as come from both Jupiter and Mercury's influence. Then one of high ennobling life and manner of manifesting same in the earth's plane. One with a high temper, yet able of controlling same and turning same into those channels wherein the better influence comes to self and others.

One, then, that gives much more to the development of others in every plane. One that has little of the influences towards detrimental conditions toward the development in the plane.

One who may, with the present will forces, make self unnecessary for return in earth's spheres.

One who, with the ennobling influences in Jupiter, brings much of this world's goods to the use of self and of others in whom there may come the influence as is seen in the mental forces.

In the development then in those adverse forces, we find one in whom many of the influence[s] of wrath and of that of the excess of the desire to hinder has at times brought consternation to the individual, yet each has been turned into that of development of self and beneficial to those whom the entity contacts.

One, then, of a loving, noble influence in lives of all whom the entity contacts. One that causes others to have faith, confidence, in self and in others. One that invites, through the radiations of unselfishness in self, the desire of others and in others to give more of their self in the earth's plane towards development.

One that finds the greater possibilities in self to give aid in every manner to others. One who would have made a *wonderful* minister in the present earth's plane. One who would have made success in ministration, or any of the developments of either economic or political forces. One that may yet in the branch of the influence towards those who labor in that of service to others, this entity may guide and direct many. This, and the usage of same, we will find the urges from appearances.

Peru

In Peru at a time when the land was submerging, he was next in power to the ruler and at the time of disaster he was especially helpful to the people. From that life came his interest in understanding the wishes and needs of groups of people, and his ability to plead their causes.

In the one before this, we find in the now Peruvian country, when the peoples were destroyed in submerging of the land. The entity then in that of the next to the ruler in the Ohlm rule, and in the name of Ormdi, and the entity then gave much to the peoples, especially to those who furnished the building of the lands for the sustenance of the peoples. In that, we find the present urge from some comes to the entity through the desire to understand the position from which any group of peoples desire their cause presented to others.

Egypt

As counselor to the ruler in Egypt, he was also a historian and carries into his present life an interest in history, especially Egyptian.

In the one before this, we find in the Egyptian forces; when the second rule that gave the peoples the laws as pertaining to the worship, the entity then in the Counselor to the then ruler, and in the name of Conraden, and was that one who assisted, especially, in the memorials as were set and placed in the land during that day, being then in the manner the historian and gatherer of data for those of that period. The present urge we find, especially, in that in the desire to know, especially, of those periods, as the entity has and will show, passed through in the earth and in other planes. The entity developed again in this.

Greece

As Xenophon, in Greece, he was said to have given people a better concept of their true nature and thus help them find within themselves more harmony and creativeness. Again he was directing groups of people. Here warring led to his present awareness of reaping whatever one sows.

In the one before this, we find [the entity] in the days of the wars in the Grecian forces. The entity then in that of him who led the forces in the raids in the Western portion of the country. Also leading the peoples to the higher understanding of self, and seeking to educate them in that which would give the better influence in their homes. Then in the name Xenophon, and in this we find in the present the urge and ability to so direct the lives of others that the best may come to them. The detrimental forces coming from these being that of the warriors of the flesh, being fearful of same.

England

From a general in Greece, the counselor later became Oliver Cromwell, fighting for the principle of personal freedom. The previous lives showed a pattern of dealing with people in large groups. In England he learned to see them as individuals. In that incarnation he developed his interest in individuals' rights and responsibilities. He also carried over his predilection for giving his best.

In the one before this we find in that of him who gave the freedom to the peoples in the English rule, when the peoples rose and sought freedom from the yoke of the King. Then in the name, Oliver Cromwell, and the entity then fought for that principle in which there was then instilled in the inmost forces, and in the present we find that urge for the ability of each individual to find their place and to fill same in their best capacity, and in this also we find that desire ever is shown in the entity to give of the best and no reserving self in any manner.

The reading ends with the prediction of a long life and with this comment on the present:

As to the abilities and how to develop same in the present, we find the entity may give much counsel to those who would serve others, and in that capacity the entity will find the greatest development for self, and the ability to do same will and is presented to the entity from time to time.   2903-1

This case illustrates a strong consistency, with the four lives all showing counseling ability, and a background of experience in dealing with large groups of people. There is a pattern of gaining through utilizing knowledge and developing abilities, and thus the demonstration of using the will.

A Christian Moslem
[2112]

... the entity has set self aright. As to what it may attain lies only within self, for kept—and keeping the faith—never would it be necessary for the entity to enter again into *this* vale, but rather to ask or journey through that presence of the faithful!
2112-1

When we look for implications in these unusual readings which volunteered the information that an individual would not need to return to the earth, can we conclude that these individuals were simply reacting in accord with benign influences brought from sojourns between lives? Did they all consistently hold firmly to their ideals, and had they been, throughout, determinedly good? This reading presents evidence that does not substantiate such conclusions.

When she came to Edgar Cayce for her life reading, this lady, a Theosophist, was employed as an apartment house manager. Her name in a previous life had been Mary Alden, and her reading got off to an unusual start. Looking for the astrological influences, the reading states that Mary's life was quite different from what it would have been, had it followed the pattern set. The reading went on to say that although there had been three stages in her development, she had so changed in the *last three or four years* because she had applied her will, that she had made wonderful strides. Consequently, this was the basis for the final comment that she could, in fact, make a return to earth unnecessary.

In entering we find the astrological influences of the entity, [2112], are quite different from that as has been *builded* in the entity in the present; for while there have been three stages of development in the present experience, those in the last three to four *years* have changed so that things that do appear in the present are but the shadow of that as would be seen from an astrological influence; for the entity has applied the will's influence in such a manner in the present—especially the latter portion of the present experience—in such a manner as to have made a *wonderful* development.

In giving, then, astrological and that builded, these must be seen can *only* be relative, and—as there has been an alteration—these must not be *confused* with developments, or with the will's influence altering the *astrological* aspect.

After this instruction not to look for the key to the personality in the planetary aspects, these influences are then listed. To a Mercury-Venus combination is attributed Mary's able mind and serene disposition. The hopefulness she manifests is explained as being a result of communion with higher levels of consciousness. Few, it is said, have gained her degree of insight into the meaning of "Seek and ye shall find, knock and it shall be opened." But her life must have its share of frustration for the reading gently admonishes her to keep her faith and commitment.

Coming under the influence of Mercury with Venus, naturally makes for a mental aptitude for the entity, but the quieting effect that the entity has upon individuals that the entity contacts is *builded* by the will's influence upon that as has become a portion *of* the entity's experience, even though the experience in Venus gives that love for peace, understanding, contentment, hope, faith, vision, long-suffering, endurance, loving kindness, and those of *brotherly* love; for these being *grounded* in that as has been experienced by the entity, the *hope* as is *manifest* in the present comes from that communion with the higher sources themselves; for he that seeks shall find, and he that knocketh to him shall be opened. Few have gained the insight into what *this* means as the entity has! Be *not* overcome with the long waiting, nor be not *weary* in well doing; for the *Master* learned obedience, even through the things which *He* suffered.

Then there is the assurance that if Mary takes good advantage of each day's opportunities, she will acquire peace, joy, and understanding. Again the reading reiterates that she should remain firm in the knowledge she has gained in *the last few years*. It reminded her, as it reminds us, that it is God who gives the increase. She would do well to work at being a channel of His blessings but without fretting about what others choose to do.

In contemplation, then, of those abilities within self, or those desires of those wanting to aid through the efforts of thine own hands—do well that thou hast in hand from day to day, and there will be given that peace, that joy, that understanding that only comes from the knowledge of God lives! And His Son is in the world! Through faith in His name may we know and see and understand all that the *physical,* the *mental,* has to bear in this mundane sphere.

In the abilities of the entity, these may only be measured by that ability of the entity to remain in that understanding, that knowledge, as has come *to* the entity in the last few years; for, as each body meets its own problems from day to day with that understanding that the increase, the love, the desires are to be kept open in a manner that is in keeping with His Son, *God* gives the increase. Be not in that position of one that frets about things, conditions, or people's not *doing* as *you* would have them do! You may only be the channel through which the reflection of His love may be made manifest for *God* works in His *own* way, own manner, and fretting self only brings those of discouragement, disillusions, as to those things that *He* would bring to pass.

Speak gently, speak kindly to those who falter. Ye know not *their* own temptation, nor the littleness of their understanding. Judge not as to this or that activity of another; rather pray that the light may shine even in *their* lives *as* it *has* in thine. These are the manners in which the sons and daughters of men may *know* His way. In this mundane sphere there comes to all that period when doubts and fears arise, even to doubting thine *own* self. These may *easily* be cast aside by knowing that He is *in* His holy temple and *all* is well.

In the conditions that come from those things that are in the past, let the dead bury their *own* dead; for *He* is the God of the living, *not* of the dead! He is Life, and Light, and Immortality! *Glory* in his weakness, *Glory* in his might, *Glory* in his watchful-loving-kindness, and *all will* be right!

Four past lives were described as affecting the present life. They have in common the fact that they were all during periods of division in the lands where they occurred. History reveals innumerable times of crisis. The air of excitement—something is happening—and the pressure to perform well or perish may be attractive to this soul. Some have built negative attitudes in a time of crisis that can only be corrected in similar stress.

Egypt

The earliest incarnation was in Egypt during a time when the

44

people were greatly divided because of disagreement over the exiling of the Priest. Mary, a priestess at the time, remained in Egypt during the exile and when the Priest returned, she aided in reestablishing the temple activities. In that life she gained because she had lived most humbly in order to adhere to her ideal. Graceful, peaceful, lovable, she was also hard-headed and set in her ways! Her fondness for ritual was traced to this life.

In the one before this we find in that land now called the Egyptian, and during that period when there were divisions in the land through the exiling of [the] Priest, through the gathering of those that made war through the divisions as were brought. The entity was then among those in the temple during the exile, remaining there, also aiding in the upbuilding when there was the return and the re-establishing. The entity was then the priestess to the Inner Shrine, making self of no estate that the *idea* as held respecting the *ideal* set by same might be kept intact. Losing in respect from many; gaining in self's own abilities to build that toward that which is set as *Right;* being hard-headed, as some would term; being set in ways, as others would call; being graceful, peaceful, lovable and law-abiding, as others would term. In the name Al-Lai, and there *still* may be seen in the holy mount—or that tomb not yet uncovered—much of that the entity made as respecting the hangings, the accoutrements for the altar in the temple of that day. In the present, that innate feeling of a certain rote, routine, and the entity is—as may ever be seen with self, with household, with others—keeping in a direct line.

The Holy Land

Incarnating again during the time of Jesus, Mary had been Selmaa, a sister of the woman at the well. During the ministry of Christ she had followed the Master, but only on the periphery. Later she became one of those who took His teachings to others. It was a life of gaining and losing—losing during the first portion when she was selfish, and gaining in the latter when she held to her ideals. It was said that certain portions of the Scripture would fill her with awe. Her present talent for needlework is traced to this experience. It is interesting to note that it is also reflective of her life in Egypt when she had helped make the temple hangings and altar cloths.

In the one before this we find in that land now called the Holy Land, and about that land where the Master walked—the entity then a sister of she whom the entity met at the well in the land, and the entity came to know of that ministry, following afar; yet later becoming one of those that spread those glad tidings to those in Mount Seir. In the name Selmaa. In this experience the entity lost and gained. Lost in the early portion when there was the aggrandizing of selfish interests; gaining in crucifying of *ideas* for ideals, and gained much through the latter portion of that experience. In the present there is felt that awe that comes with the hearing of that particular portion of the Scripture, the Gospel, the Message read, of the journey *through* that land; and the *abilities* with the needle.

Palestine

The next life was again in the Holy Land, but this time as a Moslem at the time when the Crusaders were bent upon imposing with the sword their religion of love. As Telulila, she retained the faith of her people but did much to aid those Crusaders who were taken prisoner. It was a life of gain because, according to the reading, she put into practice what she had learned in previous lives. The vignette infers an ironic comparison about the relative Christianity of the Moslem girl and the Crusaders.

In the one before this we find that land, that period, when there were contentions, wars and rumors of wars in those lands that were overrun by the peoples who—zealous of their beliefs—came into the land to conquer it. The entity was then among those in the household of that called the Moslems, and while the entity held to those tenets of the fathers in the experience, yet the entity offered much aid and succor to those who became—as they were—the *prisoners* of that people. The entity then was in the name Telulila. In this experience the entity *gained* throughout, holding to that as taught put into practice that as had been gained in the inner self through *another* association. In the contact with individuals the entity gave that as was *inmost* in self as truth. In the present has come those influences over that has held the entity to those of a high ideal as to moral, material, and spiritual laws.

New England

The time of the witch-hunts around Salem, Massachusetts, is the setting for the entity's appearance as Mary Alden. The gain it afforded her was not unmitigated. Because Mary was in the home of one of the girls persecuted, she allowed herself to develop a great animosity toward those who brought bodily suffering to those she loved. Although she had ministered well to those wounded and captured Crusaders in her Moslem life, perhaps she was attempting to learn what the readings call "loving indifference" by entering into circumstances where those needing aid and support were dear to her. But instead of giving them all of her attention, she turned, in wrath, toward those doing the persecutions. The life as Mary Alden changed her ideas about orthodox religion. This surfaces in her present interest in Theosophy.

In the one before this we find in that land now known as the Eastern or New England land, where those persecutions came for those who had the visions of the familiar spirits, or for those who saw those that walked in the shadow land. The entity was then among those who were of the household of one who suffered in the body for the *persecutions* as were brought to the household. In the name Mary Alden. The entity gained and lost through this experience, for when persecutions came, hardships came upon the entity and there were grudges held against those who brought bodily suffering to the loved ones of the entity. In the present there has ever been innate an awe to the entity of those who were teachers, ministers, preachers, or those who professed *any* association with unseen sources, and a dread to know the *end* of such! Also this has brought about much of that that has changed the entity *in* understanding as to following what has been *ordinarily* termed orthodox forces, or religious beliefs.

These lives in the earth were influential, there is no doubt. Obvious in most of them is total commitment to the highest ideal, and the carrying of that ideal from life to life.

In the abilities of the entity in the present, and that to which it may attain:
As has been given, the entity has set self aright. As to what it may attain lies only with self, for kept—and keeping the faith—never would it be necessary for the entity to enter again into *this* vale, but rather to bask or journey through that presence of the faithful!   2112-1

Neither the earth lives, nor the astrological influences were more influential than her own will. It was this that had brought her to the promise at the end of her reading.

A Doctor
[444]

. . . it is not what mind knows but what the mind applies about that it knows, that makes for soul, mental or material advancements.   444-1

A bright and talented woman, the good doctor became well known for her work in psychiatry, especially the use of art therapy in studying the emotional problems of both children and adults. This is another reading which illustrates a strong career pattern, showing several lives in medicine and healing, and others in which an objective, analytical approach was developed. Introducing the astrological influences, the reading acknowledged the importance to Dr. Beldon of her past lives, saying that her mental urges were more the results of them than of the position of the planets.

In giving that which may be helpful to the entity in the present, the approach to the astrological influences would be from the sojourns rather than the position of the planets or the elements in same. For, the sojourns make for innate influences; while the earth's appearances make for the greater *urge* within the present mental forces of the entity.

The reading mentions dual interests, which are demonstrated by her listing "artist, M.D., psychiatrist and educator." It points to her curiosity concerning the mystical and suggests that she might become a writer. The latter part of the segment dealing with the influence of Jupiter illustrates an innate aptitude for her chosen profession, psychiatry.

In this entity [444] we find rather unusual developments in the astrological influences; for these are rather as *two* urges in the inner being of the entity, or are rather in pairs. So, there will be seen in the present experience that there are periods when there have often been halting opinions or urges leading in separate directions at or during the same period of activity in the physical experience of the entity.

We find that Venus with Uranus make for rather at times the complications as to the character of associations, the activities in the relationships to those influences which are accredited to the activities of an indwelling in such environ. Hence the mystic, the occult, with love's influence, are of particular interest. Hence the entity's abilities in building or making or writing stories pertaining to activities in these directions might be developed in those periods particularly when there is the conjunction of, or the influence direct in the earth from Venus and Uranus experience.

In the activity also in Jupiter do we find the entity's indwelling, making for innate urges in the activity of the entity through those influences that make for travel, for meeting of individuals in the varied walks of life, in those that find expressions in the activity with the mental proclivities of the individual. Rather does the entity innately deal with mental and mind than with things, yet conditions as produced by the mental association and activity of individuals are of particular interest to the entity.

Atlantis

Interest in developing the perfect physical body started in the earliest life given, in Atlantis. In that life Dr. Beldon both gained and lost, lost by getting overly sexually involved with others in the temple, gained in disseminating truths. The reading suggests that by turning within she could draw on her experiences in Atlantis to write stories.

Before this we find the entity was in those experiences in the Atlantean land, before those periods of the second upheavals or before the lands were divided into the isles.
The entity was among those of the household of the leaders of the One, and made for and aided in the attempts to establish for those that were developing or incoming from the thought forces into physical manifestations to gain the concept of what their activities should be to develop towards a perfection in physical body, losing many of those appurtenances that made for hindrances for the better activities in the experience. The entity then was in the name Asme, as would be put in the language of the day. And the entity gained and lost in the experience. For, while in the office of the priestess in the temple of the One, the entity lost in the associations of the carnal influences in relationships to those in the same activity. Yet, the entity gained in the greater portion of the abilities to make for disseminating truths to others.
In the present also may come, by turning within, from that experience, that which may make for the background of many of those experiences in the writings or in the stories or in the impressions that may be had as illustrative to those whom the entity would teach.

Egypt

Interest in perfecting the physical body begun in Atlantis was also the main theme of a life in Egypt. In her life there, Dr. Beldon had worked in the Temple of Sacrifice which was much like a hospital, and was a significant part of the work of the Priest Ra Ta to purify the race. It was there that the assorted monstrosities (recorded in myths) received mental and physical treatment. At that time Dr. Beldon was active in teaching spiritual truth and helping to lay the foundation for today's medical practice.

Before this we find the entity was in that land now known as the Egyptian, during those experiences when there were turmoils and strifes through the rebellions that arose in those activities in that land, when there had been the banishment of the priest in the spiritual life—and the uprisings of the natives and those people that had sojourned in the land, and the differentiations that arose from those tenets that were being proclaimed by those incoming from the Atlantean land.

The entity then was among those that aided in re-establishing the priest among the peoples, and was of those that aided specifically in the Temples of Sacrifice of that period. Not where offerings were made of animals or of the influence or increasing of the field, but where rather those things were shifted from individual's experience, mentally and materially, that prevented their becoming more in accord with the laws that were proclaimed by the priest—aided and abetted by the activities of those that came in from the Atlantean land to establish what was in the period the greater understanding of the law of the relationships of souls to the Creative Forces, and of the individual's obligations and relations to the fellow man.

Throughout the experience the entity developed in soul, and met many of those that were antagonistic to the influencing for the betterment and many of those through whom the tenets came for the activities in giving and spreading to the peoples that which was helpful in their relationships, their experiences. The entity was particularly active in the latter portion, given to disseminating those that were of the fields of activity in what became or is the basis of much in modern medicine.

Germany

The next life was important in the developing of this physician's mental and emotional makeup. Details and specifics are sparse, but it was during the time of the Crusades and most probably in Germany. Left at home while the other members of the family trotted off with lance and shield to wrest the Holy Land from the Saracen, she evidently wrestled and fell victim to bitterness. As she faced the daily demands of life she questioned the disparities between obligations and ideals. She is said to have lost in this way, although she gained in the latter portion of the life when she gave herself in service to others.

The analytical mind Dr. Beldon has in the present is said to be directly traceable to this life at the time of the Crusades. This ability to analyze other people's problems and experiences and offer help is obviously invaluable to a psychiatrist. In that life she learned that it is not what a person knows, but what he does about what he knows that makes for advancements.

Before this we find the entity was during that period when

there were the activities of those that came into the land of promise as Crusaders for a cause, in the ideas of many.

The entity then was of the people in the Fatherland, as may be called, that were among those left by the other members of the household; and much of the duties and activities in material things fell upon the shoulders or activities of the entity in the experience, bringing to the entity many questions as to duty and obligation to those influences in the actual experience and duties and obligations that arise from impelling influences or urges to become active in or for an ideal.

Through the experience the entity may be said to have lost and gained, for there was much turmoil in the mental forces of the entity during the period, much of those experiences that made for the realizing of the necessities of material activities in a material world. Yet, in the latter portion, as in those experiences when self lost self—as it were—in that it gave to others, in the character of conditions that made for the losing of self in service to others, developments came to the entity. The name then was Herzenderf.

The entity in the experience made for those activities that in the present at times have caused the *wondering* as to the abilities of differentiation—in the experience of self—between that of practical value in the experiences of man or of self and that having more to do with the urge to the emotional influences that make for the forming of ideas, rather than ideals; or as to whether the ideals are of such standards that both the emotional and the practical influence in material things weigh well in the balance of the activities of the individuals through which the relationships bring those influences in their lives and their experience.

Hence the entity naturally in the present is of an analytical mind, with the abilities to use or apply self in analyzing others' influences or experiences in such a way as to be beneficial to such individuals who make overtures to the entity in any manner for aid in this direction. And *well* may the entity apply this experience, for not only self-development but in giving out to others those things that may be most helpful in their experience. For, the entity learned in that experience, in that land, it is not what a mind *knows* but what the mind applies or does about that it knows, that makes for soul, mental or material advancements.

Early America

The last life given places Dr. Beldon in Salem at the time of the witchcraft trials, but not personally involved in what was going on. Once again her interest was focused on the mental forces (that were making the spiritualistic manifestations

51

possible). For her, this was a very large case study; she could analyze its causes but not offer suitable assistance.

Before this we find the entity was during those periods in the present land of nativity when there was an expression of those influences in the spiritualistic realm, in and about those places in Salem, when there were the students and the persecution of those that made for activities in that particular experience.

During the sojourn the entity gained much by the physical activities in following much that was presented in the appearance of those particular phenomena manifested by those felt by many during the period as being possessed.

The entity was rather the observer than associating self with the activities during the period, and was in the name Beldon.

From that experience in the present sojourn there are seen in the activities of the entity those things pertaining to following the *mental* forces of those that are active in such fields make for the greater expression of manifestation to the entity.

The fields of reading, the fields of activity in the social relationships, arise from experiences in that sojourn.

The reading ends advising Dr. Beldon to apply the highest ideals in all of her contacts day by day. If she does so she can develop in this life to the point where she will not need to reincarnate in the earth again unless she so chooses.

As to the abilities of the entity and that to which it may attain in the present, and how:

In those fields of activity as indicated, if the entity will apply self in those forces that make for the creating within self and those whom the entity may contact day by day, ideals that are of the standards making for creative influences in the mind, the soul and the physical influences, through same may the entity gain and develop in this experience to those influences where only through the desire may it be necessary for the entity to enter earth's environs again.

Then, present self to those influences that make for creative activities in such a manner that self may never fear to meet that it has spoken in word, or thought; for each soul meets that it has meted, with those measures with which it has meted out.   444-1

By bringing to people the concept of basing their lives on an ideal rather than goals, her concern for harmonious activities of the mind could reach fruition. Then she could either return again to earth and spread her creative message further, or travel beyond this solar system in search of new challenges.

A Teacher
[1472]

Then only as an individual gives itself in service
does it become aware.   1472-1

In her incarnation in Palestine this lady's name was Judy, and her reading is filled with personal encouragement. It explains that she has come a long way and often grows weary carrying not only her own burdens, but also the burdens of those around her. She is assured that what she faces is necessary for her soul growth. The first part of the reading contains statements that should be inspirational to all, for it explains that what one does about one's life builds conditions into one's future.

These are beautiful in many of the experiences yet the more turmoil may appear to be present in this present sojourn.

For the entity has come a long way, and oft grows weary with the burdens not only that become a part of self's experience but that apparently are unburdened and yet burdened upon the entity, in its dealings with those about self.

Remember, though, that these *are* but that which is a part of the experience; for those whom He loveth, those He holdeth dear in their dealings with the fellow man.

For He hath indeed given His angel charge concerning thee, and He will bear thee up—if ye will faint not but hold to that purpose whereunto thou hast purposed in thy tabernacle in the present.

For know that His temple in thee is *holy;* and thy body-mind is indeed the temple of the living God.

Thus may ye find oft that upon the horns of the altar many of the burdens may be laid aside, and that the sweet incense of faith and hope and prudence and *patience* will arise to bring the consciousness and the awakening of the glories that may be thine.

In giving, for this entity, the interpretations of the records made—upon time and space from God's book of remembrance—we find life, as a whole, is a continuous thing; emanating from power, energy, God-Consciousness, ever.

And as it must ever be, so has it ever been; so that only a small vista or vision may be taken here and there, from the experiences of the entity in those environs of an astrological nature (as ye term).

Or the experiences of the visitation of the soul-entity, as it were, during those periods when absent from the material, three-dimensional matter, become as in the accord with what has been accredited by the students—yea, by the seers of old—to those astrological aspects.

53

That is, the influences or environs to the entity, in those consciousnesses that are given as a portion of the experience, from such sojourns, are as signs or symbols or emblems in the experience of the entity in the present.

For as the entity experiences, it is ever the *now* and what the entity or soul may do *about* the consciousness or awareness that makes for those influences which are to be.

Hence such influences that are accredited much to the astrological aspects become a portion of the entity, not because of the position at the time of birth but because of the entity's sojourn there. Or, rather, because the All-Wise, All-Creative Force has given into the keeping of the souls that they journey as it were from experience or awareness or consciousness to consciousness, that they—as a portion of the whole—may become aware of same.

And as the injunction has been from the beginning, subdue ye the influences from without, that ye may be a fit companion, that you may be one with that Creative Force or Energy ye worship as thy Maker, thy God, thy Brother—yea, that within which ye live, ye move, ye have your being!

Then, as we find, as the consciousness is aware of the individual now, and knows itself to be itself—these are the purposes.

Then only as an individual gives itself in service does it become aware. For as the divine love has manifested, does become manifested, that alone ye have given away do ye possess. That *alone* is the manner in which the growth, the awareness, the consciousness grows to be.

For until the experiences are thine, thy awareness cannot be complete.

Although few lives in the earth plane were said to be affecting Judy's present experience, there were a number of astrological aspects influencing her. Not only does she have Venus and Jupiter with their predisposition to love and beauty, but also Mars bringing expressions of anger, resentment and selfishness. She is told this influence will dissipate as she applies love in dealing with others. Also listed are Uranus and Neptune which evidently cause the turmoils mentioned in the first paragraph. These two forces represent the extremes, but they promote purification.

As to the astrological aspects, we find these become as innate or mental—or dream, or visions, or cries, or voices as it were from within.

But the influences that arise from the few appearances in the material sojourns or consciousness (that have an effect in the present) are to create or bring about or affect the emotions.

Hence as there are those contacts with individual entities—for this entity is struggling even as they—there comes with the awareness of their thought-expression in material consciousness the emotions, the awareness of their struggles having been as parallel, or at cross-purposes here or there.

Yet having left as it were upon the skein of time and space that consciousness that only in the patience of the divine love may that hope, that helpfulness be made complete—as ye lean upon the arm of thy Brother, thy Friend, ye may be borne to the very presence of divinity itself.

In the astrological aspects then we find these as a part of this entity's experience; that Jupiter, Mars, Venus, Uranus, Neptune all become a portion of the entity's innate activity.

Hence these come into material manifestation by the application of, or doing something about, the urge produced by that activity that is latent yet is so subtle, yet so definite as to produce that which brings movement to the experience of self.

Thus it becomes a portion of its activity in the material sojourn.

Venus and Jupiter bring sympathy, love, beauty; and those abilities to depict same into material activity such that it becomes a portion of the longings and the hopes of the many.

For as thoughts are things, and as their currents run into the experience of individuals, they shape lives and activities so that they become miracles or crimes in the experiences of others as they mete them in their associations with their fellow men.

For as ye do it unto the least of these, thy brethren, ye do it unto thy Maker.

Hence these make for those activities in the experience of this entity's soul in which the masses, as well as classes and groups, are to be, will be, influenced.

Hence is there little wonder that oft there is the second thought—yea, the counsel with the inner self—as to whether that written, that spoken, that printed, that said in thy dealings with others becomes as a wonderment or is constructive or destructive?

But more and more may the thoughts expressed and given out by the entity bring constructive activity in the lives of others, as the self gains that open consciousness that He has given His angels charge lest ye dash thy foot against a stone.

Hence know that He is in His holy temple, and that all the earth must hear, must know. For every knee must bow to that love divine, as ye are capable of meting and measuring through such activities in thy experience and thy relationships with thy fellow man.

In Mars we find those fits of anger, resentment, selfishness here and there; those impure motives creating those struggles, those entanglements, those angers. Yet these as they arise upon thy horizon of activity in thy relationships may oft keep from view the visions of that glory prepared for those who love the Lord.

Yet know that truth and light, as may be aroused or made

alive from the assurances of His walks with thee, will dissipate those fogs, those mists, as ye apply love in thy dealings with every character of circumstance in thy experience with others.

Then these will matter little; for the Lord's ways are not past finding out, yet ye must oft learn to wait upon the Lord, and not become overanxious—in thy anxiety that "they, too" taste of the goodness that may be found in the divine love.

In Uranus, as well as in Neptune, we find the water—yea, the elementals; the fire and water—oft interfering? no, cleansing rather. For as hath been given, all must be tried so as by fire. All must be purified.

Yet in the beauty of Life springing anew in the water of life itself, ye find in the mysteries—yea, the occult and spiritual forces—influences that make for *extremes* in the lives of many.

Yet as He [Jesus] walked the path to Gethsemane, as He struggled alone with His own Cross; so ye—as ye struggle— *have* the assurance that His presence abideth; and they that become overzealous or overanxious may find that the stepping-stones that may be in thy experience become stumbling stones.

But keep ye the faith in not the Cross as sacrifice but as the Cross as the *Way,* the *Light,* the *Life!*

For without the Cross there is not the Crown!

Egypt

In prehistoric times, Judy had been a Carpathian princess who went to Egypt to study the mysteries. She is said to have been the "first of the pure white of that land" to seek out the Priest and the Temple Beautiful in order to purify herself and take home to her people not only the spiritual truths being taught in Egypt, but also their practical application.

Before that we find the entity was in the Egyptian land, during those periods when there were the gatherings of those from the turmoils, from the banishments, and those from the Atlantean land.

The entity then was among those from lands that were later called the Parthenian lands, or what ye know as the Persian land from which the conquerors then of Egypt had come.

As a Princess from that land the entity came to study the mysteries for the service it might give to those of her own land, the Carpathians—or as has been given, the entity was among the *first* of the pure white from that land to seek from the Priest and those activities in the Temple Beautiful for the purifying of self that she, too, might give to her own people not only the tenets but the practical application of that which would bring home in the material experience an *assurance* in the separations from the body.

Palestine

Preparation in the temple under the Priest Ra Ta led to her expression as a prophetess in Palestine during the time of Jesus. An important member of the Essenes community, her name was Judy. Although, even then, she was often weary of the world's problems, the reading says she gained throughout. To that particular sojourn she owes her ability to put spiritual truth into lessons that drive a point home.

Before that we find the entity was in the Palestine land, during those days when the Master walked in the earth; and when there were the peoples about those activities of not only the birth but His sojourns before and after the return from Egypt—those whom Judy blessed, that labored in the preserving of the records of *His* activities as the Child; the activities of the Wise Men, the Essenes and the groups to which Judy had been the prophetess, the healer, the writer, the recorder—for all of these groups.

And though questioned or scoffed by the Roman rulers and the tax gatherers, and especially those that made for the levying or the providing for those activities for the taxation, the entity gained throughout.

Though the heart and body was often weary from the toils of the day, and the very imprudence—yea, the very selfishness of others for the aggrandizing of their bodies rather than their souls or minds seeking development, the entity grew in grace, in knowledge, in understanding.

And in the present those abilities arise from its desire, from its hopes to put into the word of the *day,* the experience of the day, in all phases of human experience, *lessons*—yea symbols, yea, tenets—that will drive as it were *home,* in those periods when the soul takes thought and counsel with itself, as to whence the experiences of the day are leading—as to whether they are leading to those activities that are the fruits of the spirit of truth and life, or to those that make for selfishness, and the aggrandizement of material appetites without thought of those things that are creative and only make the pure growths within the experience of others.

Hence whether it be in jest, in stories, in song or poem, or whether in skits that may show the home life, the lover—yea, the weary traveler—yea, the high-minded, and they that think better of themselves than they ought to think—*these* abilities are there. Use them. For He, even as then, will bless thee with His presence in same. And what greater assurance can there be in the experience of any soul than to know that He—yea, the Son of Mary—yea, the Son of the Father, the Maker of heaven and earth, the Giver of all good gifts—will be thy right hand, yea thy heart, thy mind, thy eye, thy heart itself—if ye will hold fast to Him!

Her most recent appearance was as Clementine in colonial America. Brought from England with the women who were to be brides of the settlers, she became part of the Byrd family, one very important in Virginia history. Because of the conditions of that life, Judy is said to resent the restriction of conventions.

Before this we find the entity was in the land of the present nativity, during those periods of the settlings in the early portions of the land.

It was when there were those being brought into the land for companions, helpmeets to those of the land.

The entity was among those brought hither from the English land, and became in the household of that family which later grew to be in authority, in power, in that Virginian land; or in the household of that family whose name has been changed to what is now called Byrd—then Bayonne [?].

In the experience, as Clementine, the entity's activities were in the assurance of the freedom of actions for the bringing not only of conveniences into the home but into the activities of the neighboring groups roundabout.

And these have left upon the consciousness of the entity such emotions that oft it finds itself bound by convention, bound by that which prevents the full expression.

Yet know in the awareness that ye will find more and more that the *truth* indeed sets one *free. Not* to convention, of the material policies or activities, but in *spirit and in truth!*

For God looks upon the purposes, the ideals of the heart, and not upon that which men call convention.

The last sentence in the reading holds the promise that *if* she will keep to the purposes as set in this life, there will be little need to return except as one who may lead the way for others. Her lives as a seeker and a teacher of spiritual truth·seemed to make this choice possible.

Thus in the abilities of the entity from that experience, as well as those gained throughout those activities, we find in the present: Just meting out day by day those visions, that ye have gained here, that ye have seen in thy experiences, thy sojourns, ye will find that *He* the keeper, *He* the Creator, will give the increase necessary for the activities in every sphere of thy experience.

For keeping inviolate that thou knowest gives assurance not only in self but in the promises that He will bear thee *up!*

If there is kept that purpose in self, there is little need for a return; save as one that may lead the way to those that are still in darkness. 1472-1

A Fiddler's Friend
[5366]

Yet may this entity be set apart.   5366-1

Studying each reading in this *Reincarnation: Unnecessary* group, I kept looking for a pattern shared by all the individuals. Every time I thought I had found one, the next case I read proved the exception. Finally I thought there might be a pattern of planets, then this reading showed up—giving no astrological influences at all. There was something ominous about the declaration that nothing would be given which might deter the entity from holding fast to her purpose, followed immediately by the suggestion that everyone present at the reading pray with the entity. Evidently there was much information in the records which was not to be told.

Excerpts from Mrs. Suthers' letter to Edgar Cayce requesting a reading, paint a picture of great physical suffering, which she later described in more detail.

10/11/43 "I have lived most of my life by knowing the power of God would keep me alive and active. At present I am taking 12 sulphur baths and massage to try to get absolutely well. My troubles now are: Right ear and Eustachian tube collapsed. Lower colon stretched very large and small passage. Tired all the time. Use of arms slows my heart, and I become exhausted standing on my feet very long. Also cannot sit down very long. Nerves down my legs hurt and pain when I lie on them or stand. Why should I come into this life with such a broken physical body? It seems I have been through hell, but an interesting trip so far, and I have often wondered what I have saved myself for. Have always wanted to be a service to humanity but no strength—angina—pernicious anemia, etc., and so on since I was young. Have I committed a great crime (murder) in the past or now—?"

The intensity of the question might have accounted for the fact that it was answered at the start of the reading. What was the cause of her physical suffering? She had been among those close to Nero, said the reading, but it immediately extended hope—"Yet may this entity be set apart." Through many experiences in the earth, it seems, Mrs. Suthers had advanced "from a low degree to one which might not even necessitate another incarnation in the earth."

Was perfection a prerequisite? Evidently not, for the reading stated that it did not mean she had reached perfection, only that there were "other realms of instruction" to which she could go. The qualifying condition was that she hold to the ideals of the Christ.

My! Some very interesting characters have been born near Bellefontaine! This entity was among those with that one who persecuted the church so thoroughly and fiddled while Rome burned. That's the reason this entity in the body has been disfigured by structural conditions. Yet may this entity be set apart. For through its experiences in the earth, it has advanced from a low degree to that which may not even necessitate a reincarnation in the earth. Not that it has reached perfection but there are realms for instruction if the entity will hold to that ideal of those whom it once scoffed at because of the pleasure materially brought in associations with those who did the persecuting.

In giving the interpretation, then, of the records of this entity, there is much that may be said but, as has been indicated, we would minimize the faults, and we would magnify the virtues. Thus may little or nothing be given that would deter the entity in any manner from holding fast to that purpose which has become that to which it may hold. For, as Joshua of old, the entity has determined (and sometimes the entity becomes very disturbed) "Others may do as they may, but as for me, I will serve the living God."

Astrological aspects would be nil in the experiences of the entity. (Let's pray with the entity.) No such may be necessary in the experience again in the earth-materiality. Remember, there are material urges and there are materials in other consciousnesses, not three dimensions alone.

Egypt

The life in Nero's court in Rome was not the only life affecting Mrs. Suthers at present, even though to it was attributed her physical condition. The earliest life was in Egypt—an incarnation she had in common with others in this group. Trained for service in the Temple Beautiful, she had been effective in helping with the establishment of homes. To that experience was credited her intense love of home and family.

Before that we find the entity was in the Egyptian land. The entity was among those who were trained in the Temple Beautiful for a service among its fellow men, contributing much to the household and the establishing of homes. Thus is the home near and dear to the entity, as are members of same, whether of the body-family or of the help or kinsmen.

Thus again may the entity find, in its application of those tenets and truths in the present, that answering in experiences of the entity in that land.

Then the entity was called Is-it-ol.

The Promised Land

The next life was at the time when the children of Israel entered the Promised Land. The seeds of desire for material things were awakened at that time. The exact circumstances seemed rather vague to me, but I was assisted by Gladys Davis Turner, Mr. Cayce's long-time secretary, who wrote an article about the case in *The Searchlight* in 1957. According to Gladys, the woman had been a daughter of Achan mentioned in Joshua 7:1 and 19. "But the children of Israel committed a trespass in the accursed thing; for Achan, the son of Carmi, the son of Zabdi, the son of Zerah, of the tribe of Judah, took the accursed thing; and the anger of Jehovah was kindled against the children of Israel." Chided by Joshua, Achan confessed to taking the spoil of silver and gold and was then stoned to death by the children of Israel—in front of his children. The shame and humiliation made a strong imprint especially since it was accompanied by suffering and deprivation as a result of the loss of her father. She clung to the belief that her father had been unjustly treated.

Before that we find the entity was in the land when the children of promise entered into the promised land when there were those whose companion or whose father sought for the gratifying of selfish desires in gold and garments and in things which would gratify only the eye. The entity was young in years and yet felt, as from those things which were told the entity, that a lack of material consideration was given the parent. The name then was Suthers.

Rome

The next life saw the desire for material pleasure brought into full bloom. Remembering that our emotional natures are the result of our lives in the earth and that we carry over our strong desires and bitterness as well as our loves, it is not hard to speculate that the deprived and embittered girl of the previous life was willing to do anything to ensure for herself a life without pain and suffering. The reading here alludes again to the association with Nero, stating that it was this particular experience for which the entity was paying with her present life of physical suffering. In her article, Gladys suggests that "as the companion or associate of Nero she would have had every opportunity to feel the emotion of 'getting even' with those who had stoned her father. Perhaps some of the Christians being persecuted were reincarnated souls who had unmercifully stoned her father—or perhaps she had personally known them before the persecution and had hated them 'without a cause' so far as could be judged in that lifetime. At any rate, as Nero's companion, she participated in the persecutions."

Before that we find the entity, as mentioned, as a companion or associate of that one who persecuted those who believed in, those who accepted faith in righteousness, in goodness, in crucifying of body desires, in crucifying the emotions which would gratify only appetites of a body, either through the physical self or through physical appetites of gormandizing, and of material desire for the arousing more of the beast in individual souls.

America

With revenge left behind, her next life, carrying its effect into the present, was one of gain and growth. Again the segment of the reading dealing with that life is open to a certain amount of interpretation. It is possible that it means she was a teacher or a missionary to the early settlers. Whatever the exact circumstances, she grew "in attempting to interpret man's relationship to the Creative Forces or God."

As to the appearances in the earth, those would only be touched on, as indicated, to be a helpful experience for the entity, as:
Before this we find the entity was in the land of the present nativity, through the experiences in seeking for new undertakings with the associations or companions. The entity became a helper to those who sought to know more of that which had been the prompting of individuals to seek freedom and to know that which is the spirit of creation or creative energies. Thus did the entity grow in attempting to interpret man's relationship to the Creative Forces or God. The name then was Jane Eyericson.

The reading lists three virtues Mrs. Suthers was demonstrating: patience, consistency, and brotherly love. Evidently the cultivation of these positive traits was helping her continue her advancement "from a low degree" alluded to in the beginning of the discourse.

As to the abilities:
Who would tell the rose how to be beautiful; who would give

to the morning sun, glory; who would tell the stars how to be beautiful? Keep that faith! which has prompted thee. Many will gain much from thy patience, thy consistence, thy brotherly love. 5366-1

Gladys Davis included the following report from Mrs. Suthers in the file:

She stated in an interview on 3/11/47 with Hugh Lynn Cayce, while he was lecturing in Boston, that since childhood she had had a serious back deformity which the doctors thought would be incurable and would eventually cause her death. It has always been a great struggle for her in meeting this condition. She also lost part of one finger at the age of four.

As a child, she remembers playing a piece of music called "Ben Hur Chariot Race." She was so fond of this that she played it over and over by the hour.

Letter 1/13/48 gave the following report as to the characteristics analyzed correctly, etc. "(1) Many accidents when young. Lost part of one finger. Hand mangled, but normalcy. (2) Trying to hold to a high ideal and help others do the same. (3) When we used to have a maid she was considered one of the family. (4) Forever grasping at and striving after perfection although falling far short. (5) When young, my mother wanted me to take music lessons because she received much satisfaction playing by ear and I had no talent. At the end of a term the music teacher dismissed me as a disgrace to her teaching. I learned quickly and easily 'The Ben Hur Chariot Race.' Played it on all occasions so fast and dramatically that it shocked all listeners. When I looked at the picture on the outside of the sheet, the charging steeds and chariots racing with the Roman Arena filled with cheering crowds, I became as one with the whole living action, was aware of nothing until I hit the final note. At 57 I think I could still play parts of it although I have not touched a piano for over 40 years. (It was the only piece I could play.)

"When in grade school and on through college, we never knew if I would live, was given up to die several times but by will power I struggled on, never complaining but in constant pain. Medicine always seemed to make me worse. Now I am almost the picture of health and younger looking than when twenty.

"Training in the Temple Beautiful must have carried over in this expression as, after graduation from the University, I took charge of a Woman's Dormitory as acting Dean. The next winter they placed me in charge of the Commons, the campus dining hall. Then following two doctors' orders I got a position in the Northwest—matron-preceptress—acting dean in a State Teachers College Dormitory. I loved the students, the buying of provisions and thinking up new ideas to help the Normal School children get warm lunches, etc.

"The reading has been a godsend in helping me to understand the whys of my struggle to exist physically and mentally. My dear mother used to say, 'You must be saved for a purpose.' My brother, M.D. specialist, said: 'Nothing seems to help you; if you live it will be because you experiment upon yourself.'

"Near death I heard 'iodine for leukemia' three nights in succession and it pleased me to read how much you have recommended it. (6) Have always hoped I would never have to live again. (7) Easily understood the cause of crime and the criminal's feeling. (8) At Ohio State University I planned houses covering a square, inner court and a tiny apartment for each one in a family so that they might live in peace. The Professor rejected all my ideas as unworkable, but he never changed my heart desire. (9) I have tried to apply all of the suggestions in the reading except about moving to the middle west. I still have much to overcome.

"May God bless your work in every way. I am sorry the two sons' readings have not seemed to help them as mine has helped me; perhaps something may be worked out for them as the years come along and their readings prove a blessing."

A Governess
[1741]

... patience, long-suffering, kindness, endurance, tolerance and brotherly love, faith, hope, charity to all. These are as the children of the entity's development ...   1741-1

In the unglamorous role of governess, this soul found a fitting opportunity to excel spiritually. The description of Lystia's personality makes her sound ideally suited for the position—soft-spoken, gentle and patient. Not only does she take time to notice and appreciate life, her presence influences others to do the same. Her reading outlines how she had built toward her present and potentially crowning earthly incarnation.

The familiar configuration of planets appears:

In entering the present experience, we have the entity coming under the influence of Uranus and Venus, Jupiter and Mercury. Hence those conditions as personalities, manifestedly building in the present entity:

One high-minded, yet the tempered thought and experience influenced by those of an occult or mystic nature; love ruling in the influences of the entity, and in the scope of mental abilities these take—especially interest—are influenced by those of the love's influence, rather than of *material* conditions, yet material forces are apparent in the influences that bring such changes in the experience of the entity, as has made for that as builds for patience, long-suffering, kindness, endurance, tolerance and brotherly love, faith, hope, charity to all. These are as the children of the entity's development, making for those influences as build in the present experience, as develops—which, when grown and manifested in the material actions of the body, bring that pleasing, patient personality as is manifested—especially with those whom the entity *would* influence; using then those armors that are rather of the nature of disarming to those that would be in a hurry, in a bluster. Not that wrath does not present itself, but rather that the influences through the *experiences* have brought that as develops the control, rather than being controlled by such for the entity.

One appreciative of literature, especially those of the descriptive nature of the outdoors and the influence that same has upon those that experience—either in reading or in actuality—such visions, such surroundings, such scenes. Patient in that of study, especially as bear an influence towards those things that bespeak of the spiritual life. While in the entity's development there are set rules for self, tolerance in others brings a *beauty* to the entity's speech and activity that draws—rather than repels—the influence of the entity. In the appreciativeness of kindnesses, soft words, gentleness, the entity may be called one as excels; making friends easily, enemies seldom; holding little grudges, yet *positive* in its ideals, in its ideas as to the approach to ideals.

One that is handy, or a handmaid in the arts of sewing, mending, or gathering together of the studies of such, and especially as brocades or laces, figures in cloth, interest the entity.

In the development, or that to which it may attain in the present, rather the application of that as has been set before self—for *well* has the way been chosen. Many depend *physically* upon, depend *mentally* upon, the activities of the entity. Be true to the duties set by self. Know that the way made is in keeping with the ideal set before self.

Atlantis

To the life as Ameer, the earliest incarnation mentioned, is attributed Lystia's inclination toward anything mystic. Many Cayce readings indicate that in Atlantis there was much experimenting, both good and bad, with the "unseen forces." It suggests that Lystia's present day caution about drugs resulted from her Atlantean sojourn. One is led to wonder whether the experimenting with drugs in the last few decades is a re-enactment from that time. Whatever the implications, the lady was clearly told that in her consciousness she was "mindful that those that are of the chemical, or chemical combines in the present, do not gain a hold that may not easily be set aside." Whether she had learned this by experience or observation is not told. Only the impression on the soul memory is stressed.

In the one before this we find in the land known as the Poseidan, or a portion of the old Atlantean. In this period the entity found much of those that pertained to the mysteries of nature, in the application of unseen forces, in the usages of same for man's indwelling, and man's physical dwelling. Hence much that is of the mystic, symbol, symbolistic, or of that as brings to the varied consciousnesses of an entity, does the entity often dwell upon; being mindful that those that are of the chemical, or chemical combines in the present, do not gain a hold that may not easily be set aside. In the name Ameer.

Egypt

Io-Li was among the royal Egyptians at the time when large numbers of people came into the country from other lands. The consternation of the natives at the onslaught of immigrants left many emotional scars that individuals carried into future lives. In this instance the woman's original rebelliousness was replaced by acceptance, so instead of an angry scar, she carried into the present an ability for self-control and an inclination to submit graciously to those in authority. The reading states that the entity had both lost and gained through the experience. In that life she bore a child who later became a most important teacher. Having been the channel for a teacher, she herself is now a teacher.

In the one before this we find in that land known as the Egyptian land, and in the days when there were the incoming of the peoples from the hill country did the entity attempt to cause those in authority to rebel; yet in the changes as were wrought—for the entity was then among those of the royalty of that period or land, in the household of the ruler in the southern portion of the land—the entity lost and gained through the experience; being then in that place that gave *to* the land a teacher, through the body that afterward became a mighty one in word, in deed, and in activity. In the name Io-Li. In the present experience this gives the entity that ability to control self, even when those conditions that are held as imperative are overridden by others in power or place.

Philippi

The life that seems to have made the strongest impression on her present life was one in Philippi. In that life her name was Lystia, and she sold lace, purple brocade and linens. A special kind of purple cloth was made by the guild of dyers at Thyatira, and it is possible that this was among her wares, for the reading says that she sat by the river among the women of Thyatira as they listened to the gospel. The reference in the reading to those from a foreign land who taught the women of Thyatira might well mean Paul, Silas and Timothy and the story in Acts 16. After learning about the "new rule or ideal" Lystia used what she heard. Her present life reflects the truths she learned and applied. Her talents for teaching and ministering and her general consideration for others stem from the high ideals set long ago as she listened by the river.

In the one before this we find the entity among those who sat by the river, as the gatherings on the feast days, and listened to the speech and the exhortation by those who gave a new message from the foreign land to the women of Thyatira and Sidon, for the entity was then a seller of lace, purple brocade and linens, and in the *city*—as of Lystra did the entity dwell—a maiden throughout the experience, and the entity gained through this experience, for much as was gained in the service set—and in the applications of the new rule or ideal as was given in this experience—did the entity apply and use in that experience. In the name Lystia. In the present, that of the aide, the teacher, the succor, the minister to the needs, the wants, of those dependent upon the activities of another, does the entity see, to find expression in that held within self's own heart.

Echoed in these lives of Lystia are the patterns of service to others and adherence to the highest ideals. Lystia's place as governess might have been considered lowly from a material standpoint, but for her spiritual development it was a fitting place. In this life, the reading asserts, Lystia has the ideal opportunity for service and may never again be drawn back to an earthly incarnation.

In the abilities of the entity in the present, as given, these may be made to excel—and the entity may so apply those tenets as have been set before self, in its ministration to those that are about the entity, that no return would be necessary in *this* experience or plane; for in *Him* is the light, and the light came among men, showing men the way to find that consciousness in *self*—for the *kingdom* is of *within,* and when self is made one *with* those forces there may be the accord as is necessary for "Come up higher. Being faithful over a few things, I will make thee ruler over many." 1741-1

An Actress
[4353]

One that is of beautiful figure and stature, and one that shows the love of the arts in every manner.
4353-4

Three physical readings preceded the life reading for this young actress, who was suffering from anemia and tuberculosis in its early stages. Attendant correspondence suggests that at the time her degree of success on the New York stage was not noteworthy. The third physical reading was especially encouraging and assured her that she would get a good part in a long-running production. It stressed the importance of following carefully all of the previously given instructions for her health, stating also:

The spiritual forces need only be given the incentive to act through the mental and the physical. Hence the necessity in this to keep the physical and the mental fit that through such work the body may develop.

The friend who had sought Cayce's help for the young lady wrote to say that her condition was much improved, and that as a result of the reading she was less despondent about her career. The young man went on to say that Venus (as we'll call her) was going to write for her horoscope (as the early life readings were called). She wanted to know what she would be when she came back next time. Her life reading is very brief, but she must have been surprised to read that she might have the choice of not ever coming back.

The astrological urges include a frequent combination of planets—Mercury, Venus and Jupiter. The picture that emerges is of a beautiful, loving girl, with a strong esthetic sense.

The mention of Arcturus among the planets indicates she previously had faced the same question of leaving this solar system and, evidently, chose to undertake more earthly challenges and incarnations.

Yes, we have the conditions and the surrounding elements in reference to the relations of this entity in the present earth's plane. We find at this time there were many that took their flight from same sphere as this, and they have, and will, manifest many of the beauties in the earth's plane in the years to come.

This entity, we find, was completed soon after the birth, and spirit and soul took its flight from Venus, with those helpful influences in Mercury and with that of Uranus and Arcturus, with variations in the Sun and in Mars and Jupiter forces. Hence many conflicting elements enter into the mind of the entity in the present earth's plane, yet all of these, with the will, may redound to the good of the entity in this earth's plane. From the position then of the planetary and systems' influence, irrespective of will, we find as these:

One that is of beautiful figure and stature, and one that shows the love of the arts in every manner. One given to give the rhythm of many, many, beautiful contributions, of others, however.

One that may love too well.

One that gets the great understanding in the Mercury influence, with Jupiter, yet one that would be called hard-headed and one that, once set against a principle, a condition, little reason, except at times, influences; yet the loving influence through the mental forces may aid the persuasion into the conditions, against the entity's better judgment. Hence the elements of conflicting conditions.

One that will find the greater work, the greater success, in the developing of the talent as is exercised in the present earth's plane. One given to represent, and express, and manifest, many of the beauties of the body and of the rhythm of life, in a manner that brings the exaltation of the work itself.

One that, when those conditions arise as given, must use the will's forces in the good, yet one, we will find, that often uses the mental forces to determine good, for with the influence in Jupiter and from Venus, with Mercury, many ennobling things are turned to destructive without mental forces are exercised [or, because the mental forces were not properly exercised], and the correct incentive carries out those conditions [correct motives would solve this problem].

The reading then assures her that her health will improve. It alludes to former readings which encouraged her to follow her acting aspirations. It also volunteers the suggestion that she postpone marriage until after she turns twenty-nine.

One that will have strong body after reaching the second cycle from the present. One that will bring many of the beauties to the world with those with whom it has been associated in other spheres.

In the vocation, follow that as has been given, and as being followed.

As to those concepts in the wedded life, better that these be deferred until the body passes age twenty-nine.

Atlantis

The earliest life mentioned was in Atlantis. Evidently she was there at the time of the destruction because later in the reading, her fear of impending danger is attributed to that life.

In the one before this in that of Poseidia, and in that Atlantean rule this entity then was in the household of the peasant that gave the information regarding the upheaval in the mountains that brought the destruction to the land.

Persia

Then to Persia—if she was in Egypt it isn't mentioned, which is unusual because each of the others had an influential incarnation there. The characteristic stemming from this life is vague. It *might* imply that she learned to live amicably with a domineering person.

In the one before this, we find in the days when the rule now in Persia was under that of Croesus, and this entity then in that of the household of the one next to the king.

Greece

Her beauty and talent as an actress came from the next incarnation, which was in Greece.

In the one before this, we find in the Grecian rule, when the lands were given to the study of body beautiful, and this entity then led in the dance of that day.

France

The latest life given was in France, and to it she owed her love of the beautiful. She loved unselfishly, and wanted the best for those close to her.

As to former appearances in the earth's plane, we find in one before this in the courts of the French, in the time of the Henry that reigned in that land, and in the court of the monarch as the favorite in that court, though not of the monarch's household.

This reading is somewhat unusual in that it carefully summarizes the traits and talents and shows to which life they may be attributed.

As to the personalities as exhibited from the individualities of this entity:
In the first, that of the fear of impending danger. These are innate conditions.
In the second, in the rule of those who would be the master of the entity; that ability to do so.
In the next, the gift of those elements through which the entity should develop itself at present.
In the next, the love of the beautiful, yet un-reserved to self, so long as those whom the entity cares for receive the best.
Then, from these, gain this understanding:
Keep in that way that the development of the soul may be such as not necessary for the return, unless the entity so desires. Then it may bring to itself those conditions in its own mental forces through which the soul gains its development.
4353-4

This is a very short life reading and given very early (1924) in Edgar Cayce's career. Past lives were mentioned, placed, but the details that would fill out the framework are not there.

An Architect
[322]

... thou hast truly shown that thou preferest thy
brother to thine own gratification!   322-2

This case is one of several in the group which illustrates a strong career pattern. An architect in his twentieth-century life, this man was well suited for his profession both astrologically and by his past lives in the earth. The reading stressed, however, that what he had accomplished in his present life was more the result of his past lives in the earth than his astrological aspects. His use of will greatly outweighed the mental urges symbolized by the planets. Mr. Pleadila (a past life name given in the reading) was told that he was very meticulous and apt with figures and would have made a good banker. He had a keen mind and was also skillful with line drawings, talents highly appropriate for an architect.

In entering, we find, from the astrological view, or from the astrological aspects, that the entity's experience in the present has not run in line with much that would be indicated in the purely astrological; while that which the entity has accomplished in the present experience has been a development from the experiences in the earth.

Yet there are those impulses that are indicated in the general mien, or manner of the entity. As in Mercury, not only from the astrological influence by indwelling but from that of the more universal aspect in the signs under which the entity was in the aspect of at birth (for these are mixed, see?).

Then, we find these rather inclining to the period or aspect that was just passed in the entity's experience, in the astrological sphere, making for:

One very neat, very particular; very apt at figures, and the entity would have done well as a banker!

In the more specific aspects from the sojourns in planetary influences and from the earth's appearances, there will be given, then, those influences both innate and manifested in the personality in the present experience:

Under Mercury, rather the high mental abilities; an aptness with lines, drawings, figures, and those things that materially have to do with such are of special interest.

The next portion of the astrological section offers an explanation of Saturn as bringing about test periods—tests which Mr. Pleadila evidently passed with flying honors. Mars also offered opportunities for learning. Under this influence he had represented the causes of minority groups, had acted as a peacemaker and managed to accomplish things in trying situations. He has demonstrated truth, veracity and clean living, therefore there will be little need *unless desired* to return to this earth's experience.

Saturn's influences have made for rather those test periods, and those experiences where the mental attitude necessary had to be expressed or manifested in order for the entity to remain steady.

Under the same influence will be seen those periods also, in the present experience, when there have been opportunities where the entity could have acted for selfish motives without being questioned by those in authority, yet for self's own high ideals the entity has rather *stood* the test; and greater will be the crown for the soul!

Those influences also in Jupiter make for rather the broad, ennobling influences that are manifest in the experience of the entity; and one called to represent, then, groups and peoples in various walks of life, in positions or places where—without other than the desire for an active service has there been remunerations.

For, we shall see these reasons in the entity's earth's experiences and their influences; for, as we have given, developments have been great in this present experience.

Also from Mars we find those active influences in those periods where, to the entity, it has meant the representing of the minority activity in relationships with others; and acting in the capacity oft rather as the peacemaker (which would be at variance, as indicated, to that which would be from the purely astrological aspect).

Not that this indicates there is no temper; nor that the entity does not find at times outlets to express the disagreements with conditions, circumstances, individuals' activities and the like; yet rather does the entity take same—and has taken same—with the air of one who does *accomplish* things, who has accomplished things, even in the trying positions in experiences with the fellow man.

Quite an enviable position, may it be said, that the entity occupies; in the matter of truth, veracity, clean *living,* that the entity has made in this experience! and there will be little need, unless desired, for a return to this earth's experience.

For, there may be those cleansings that will make for, "Come thou and enjoy rather the glory of thy Lord, for it may be said thou hast truly shown that thou preferest thy brother to thine own gratification!"

The man has accomplished much in this life, largely as a result of his experiences in the earth. We look at the earliest life to see the start of the pattern.

Egypt

In pre-historic Egypt, the entity we call Mr. Pleadila worked closely with the king who built the pyramids and had supervised their building. He was told that seeing them today would not only arouse a feeling of awe but would also remind him, if only subliminally, of the truths taught in that life. To that life he can attribute a greater understanding of the relationships of body, mind and spirit.

In the one before this, we find that the entity was in that land now known as the Egyptian, during those periods when there was the establishing of those tenets that had been broken down through the rebellions which had arisen.

The entity then acted in the capacity to the king who *builded* those temples that spread to that *now* known as the pyramids, rather the obelisks [?], and those of the varied standards in columns.

And if the entity but gazes upon those builded—by self, even, or under self's supervision—there comes the feeling of awe in the present; not only from what those meant to the entity during the experience, but the constant harking—mentally, spiritually—to those tenets through that experience, as Apt-Henri.

In the present there may be that added also, from the experience of that sojourn, that may bring to the activities of the entity a *greater* understanding in the relationships of material, and mental, and spiritual affairs.

Samaria

The next life given was in Gadara in Samaria at the time when Jesus was teaching there. We notice that once again he was connected with government, and see also that the universal truths which he had learned earlier in Egypt prepared him for the truth taught by the Master. We see him first as the chief of counsel to the police. Evidently, when he accepted the teachings of Jesus, there was some dissension around him and he was falsely accused, perhaps of embezzlement. Although this caused him great mental anguish, he was able to use his carefully kept records to prove his innocence. The reading suggests that his accuracy is a result of that experience, as is tenacious holding to his ideals.

In the one before this we find that the entity was during that period when the Master walked in the land, and the entity was then among those of the citizenry in the Samaritan land, in Gadara, when the people of that city came to hear, to understand, that taught those by the well.

The entity then was among those that acted in the capacity of what would today be called the chief of counsel to the police, or those that kept order; known then among the elders of the land, and in the name Pleadila.

In this experience the entity gained and lost; gained throughout those periods of activity in the official capacities. With the accepting of the teachings, and when there arose dissensions, the entity was falsely accused of turning divers positions, divers solutions, into self's own interests, and faults arose—or the judging that arose brought *suffering* in the mental; yet satisfaction and strength when the entity was able to *prove* through those records made, that all *was* right.

Is it any wonder, then, the tediousy or accuracy with which the entity makes marks? or bespeaks that which is nearest and dearest to the ideals of self?

Out of office, he then became a teacher and one who helped in the building of a city. As a result of the life in Samaria he is drawn to those who interpret the teachings of Jesus, and feels that mercy, hope, justice, peace and harmony bring the greatest rewards even in adverse circumstances.

The entity then became a teacher, and one who aided in the establishing and building of a city—alone—separate from those, even of the peoples of that particular land.

In that experience the entity became an old patriarch, living to be an hundred and nine years of age.

From that experience in the present the entity also finds a constant drawing towards those that counsel as to the teachings, and interpretations of the teachings, of the man of Galilee.

In the present also is there found the close adherence to that innately felt from the experience, that mercy, hope, justice, peace and harmony bring the greater reward, even under stress or strain, than dwelling in the tents of the wicked for a little while.

Early America

Again we see Mr. Pleadila involved in government, as an aide to either governors or to a governing body at such time as civil and moral laws were being studied. Not only did he assist in influencing the kind of government to be established but he also assisted in laying out the grounds of the city on Manhattan Island, as well as in upstate New York. The readings said that his current inclination to architecture was the result of that life, but we recall that he'd had experience in building a city in a previous life.

He was told that the life in early America might help him to be a judge of antiques, largely because of the memories that those antiques would awaken in him. There is a seeming bit of precognition in this segment. It states that the country was going to come into a period of interest in early American decor. The reading was given in 1933 but it was not until the late nineteen forties that such a trend did begin.

In the one before this we find that the entity was during those periods when there were the establishings, in the land of the present nativity, the first forms of government that pertained to the consideration of the generations yet to come.

The entity then was among those who acted in the capacity as an aide to those that governed those peoples, and made for the rules and regulations that governed not only the moral relationships but the civil relationships also, and those conditions that pertained to the establishing of homes.

Then the entity was in the name of Lanfard. In the records

that may be found among the forms of government which followed Stuyvesant's rule, there may be found much that was accomplished by the entity through that experience.

For, the entity assisted in not only the *character* of the structure (as to law, and civil relationships and moral relationships), but in that of engineering or laying out the grounds, putting the metes and bounds about those various lands that were settled on the island, as well as farther up the State.

From this experience has come that inclination in the present for lines, for figures, for those things pertaining to architectural drawings, and those things pertaining to characterization in homes and furnishings also.

And, *especially* as a judge of antiques and the part they played, or *may* play in the affairs of individuals, would the entity in these periods be able—or be given an opportunity—to awaken much that has been *innate* in the entity's experience.

For, the periods in America are turning to more of the colonial or *early* American nature. And the entity had much to do with those very conditions that *broke* away from the homeland or foreign activity that had been adhered to; in the furniture, furnishings, frames, moldings, finishings within the home, etc.

In this line, with that position the entity *now* occupies, much may be accomplished.

The very end of the reading reiterates the advice:

As to the abilities in the present, then, and that to which the entity may attain:

As we have given, in the ways of the Lord follow close. These are ever before thee, in the mental and the material relations.

In the material, add—to those in the present activity—that of judging, counseling, for those that would create or gather together those representations of the early periods in the *American* life. 322-2

While career patterns are strong in this reading so is the pattern of consistently living up to the highest ideals, regardless of circumstance, ever preferring his brother to himself. Now, according to his reading, he is in "quite an enviable position."

A Mother to All
[404]

... those who have come under the influence of the entity will—at *some* period in *their* experience— have been glad to have known the entity. 404-1

The reading states specifically that this lady is one of few of whom it can be said that she will not need to reincarnate, and the statement appears twice. Her name was Hannah and the personality described by the astrological aspects given is a beautiful one. She is pictured as loving, cheerful, and calm—being a mother to all and having the ability to make ends meet. She could well have been a nurse or counselor. She was active in the A.R.E. until her death at the age of 75 in 1965. A warm and inspiring person, she was widely loved.

In entering this experience, we find the entity coming under the influences astrologically, through sojourn as well as relatively in this present experience, of Venus, Jupiter, Uranus, Mercury, with those influences as make for the planetary associations with that as known in the present as the astrological in Leo and in that as makes for changes and alterings in the application of individual or entity's will as respecting these influences.

In this present we see rather as a warning for the entity respecting an accident that might be in the experience of the entity in October of the present year. Be mindful through the early portions, especially, of that period; for at that period we will have conjunctions of influences as have acted upon the entity as respecting the application of will, and will bring then a relative influence in that period.

Under Venus we find that influence as makes for, in the present personality of the entity, one loving in mien, and as a mother to many, as giving that influence in those contacted by the entity, as causing each to think more of their duties and obligations in these directions and their relationships to others.

In Jupiter we find those influences as make for a broadening of scope, a student, a delver into many varied experiences for self and the experiences of others, gathering from same a little here, a little there, as to the application of those truths or experiences gained in those influences in the life.

One that makes for also that adaptability of self to the varying circumstances as arise in the experiences of the entity in its *daily* life in this experience.

In Uranian influences we find those that make for an *unusual* experience in this particular entity, for it acts rather as that of the *balancing* of self in varied experiences; where others lose either their temper or judgment, the entity remains as calm and easy through the experience, through that influence as had by entity under this astrological sojourn.

In Mercury we find that ability to make ends meet, as it were, in the various experiences, by being capable, able, to counsel with, in, a lighter vein; apparent to others that often the entity hasn't delved *into* that as is worrying them. To the entity this experience gives the ability to enable others to pass, as it were, under the rod in an *even* tone. Well would the entity, had a choosing been of making for self an ability, that of the nurse—or of the counselor, or the directress of groups that were hard to understand by others.

In that *builded,* as we find, in the *present* experiences through these as given:

One capable of meeting those conditions in life in a cheery, affable and easy manner, apparently to others; yet that inflicted upon self through the meeting of same has its effect upon the whole of the *building* of the entity, and that may be said of *this* entity as of few we find through this experience—that may be builded in the present that will not require the entering into the earth's experience again; for much has been builded through the experiences in the earth's plane, and the sojourns have been those that have added to that, that to those who have come under the influence *of* the entity will—at *some* period in *their* experience—have been glad to have known the entity.

Peru

The earliest life given was one in Peru at the time refugees were arriving there from Atlantis. Although she was a priestess at the time, the reading says she lost because she resented the newcomers and did not make things easy for them. Present day fears of possible calamities are said to be traceable to this life. She was advised to alleviate those nameless fears with prayer.

In the one before this we find in that land now known as the Peruvian land, and in the days of the Ohms [Aymaras?] when there were the coming in of the peoples from the Poseidan land, and from the Eizen [?] land. The entity was then among those that were of the priestesses of the land. The entity lost through a greater portion of this experience in making for hardships to those who came, as it were, seeking for aid and succor as the lands they left were being destroyed. In the name Zuze. In the present, fear often enters the entity's *inmost* self through calamities that are apparent—or through those things that might happen which often never do. In *this* the entity will find that in seeking to that same source through which the entity attained much in the Egyptian experience, may fear be cast aside.

Egypt

In her life in Egypt, Hannah was a sister to the Priest, Ra Ta. She went with him into banishment, holding true to her ideals and bearing no resentment. At that time she was something of a baker, supplying cakes for the various altars. The reading

78

says she ministered to the physical and spiritual needs of those who gathered in the temples. Unleavened cakes were evidently buried with the dead at that time and the reading states that some of those baked by Hannah may still be found.

Although she gained through most of that experience, she lost in the latter part when the King tried to put someone else in the Priest's place.

In the one before this we find in that land now known as the Egyptian, and during that period when there were trials and turmoils through the variations as were brought in the experiences of the peoples through the banishment of the Priest, and the turmoils and strifes that arose within the groups. The entity was then among those of the Priest's own household, and a sister then to the Priest, going in banishment with those as were sent into the southern land; not even holding a grudge, yet true to that as felt by the entity as the *ideal* of an *idealist* at that period. The waywardness, the faults, the entity saw—but counted to *her* as *good* to remain in the counsel of those that were able to approach the *greater* force or source of powers as made manifest in that period. In the name As-Razh. In those places yet uncovered may much of that as was accomplished by the entity in the period be yet found, even the cakes of unleavened bread as were buried with those of that period made by the entity *still* be found intact. The entity in the experience was one that supplied those of the cakes of the various characters to the various altars, as well as ministering to the *physical* and *spiritual* needs of those that gathered in the temples—either as a portion of the mental worship, or as favorites to the King, or as favorites to those in power in that experience. The entity gained through the greater portion of this experience, losing only when in the latter days there was the attempt to again put others in power where the priest *had ruled,* or governed, the entity *rebelled* against that attempt on the part of the *King* and those in power of the native rules. In this the entity found those of the sources of contempt, yet those peoples to the latter days of the entity served much and held the entity high, and those that later became as the symbol to the Egyptians, with the hawk, with the woman's face—or the woman with the hawk's face—are from the activities of the entity in a much *earlier* experience.

The Promised Land

Hannah was with the children of Israel, when they made their pilgrimage out of Egypt into the Promised Land. In that life she gained because, regardless of the hardships of both the bondage and the journey, she remained true to the highest of ideals. As a result of this life she is very much interested in

79

travel and understands why some people just collapse under trial. Also to this life is attributed her ability to remain cheerful when slighted, and the reading repeats that she is a mother to all.

In the one before this we find during that period known as the return of the peoples to the promised land from that land of bondage, as the peoples were led from the pilgrimage into the promised land. As has been recorded, *few* that were of the age of accountability entered in the promised land. The entity *then, again* in the name of Hannah, left Egypt and entered in the promised land; in the household of those that settled in their division of the land about Bethel. In this experience the entity gained, for though the hardships of bondage—as well as those of the following through the various experiences in the journeys—the entity held to that ideal, that that had *builded* the promise in this particular people, in this particular period. In the present, this and other sojourns—or travel—are of special interest to the entity, and while others wonder often at the falling away of the peoples under the various experiences and the various trials that arose, to the entity these are easily—or more easily—understood than to many. In this application in the present, the abilities to counsel with, to reason with, the cheeriness of an often counted slight rather makes for a variation in the *experience* of those whom the entity contacts, and a mother to all.

Norway

In Norway Hannah was the mother of Eric the Great (who once again is her son). The tie to the sea seems to be a continuing one, for her husband in this life was a captain who went to sea as a cabin boy at the age of eleven. The reading points out that Hannah learns something from every experience and applies what she learns to the next experience.

In the one, then, before this we find in that land known as the Norse land, and during that period when there were the sailings for the foreign or the unknown shores. The entity then was the mother of Ericsson the Great, that sailed the uncharted seas, and again is that in the keeping of that entity, in the son [2157?], and he again will lead many through *that* direction, through that care, that attention as *has* been, *is* being, *will* be given by the entity's own *individuality;* for these bespeak of those things that build for a continuity of forces in the entity's experience. In the present from this experience the entity finds, that whatever may be that as is experienced must have *in* same that which—*if* sought—will be an aid to meet the *other* conditions as they arise. *Well,* and a developing influence.

80

The end of the reading reiterates the information that in this life she could reach the point where she would not be required to reincarnate in the earth again.

In the abilities of the entity in the present and that to which it may attain, and how:
As has been seen, as has been given, in the present there may be attained that which will not require the entering into the earth's experience, but rather as the journeying on to those of the higher realms in which the entity may express or manifest self in that as has been gained.
As to how, in meeting those exigencies as they arise from day to day, keeping the heart, the mind, *singing* in the glory of that that was made manifest in Him who came as the light and the life, that through Him all might find the door to enter in; for *He* is the way, the truth *and* the light, and as the entity—through the varied experiences not here given, as the entity through those experiences given—found that in Him *as* the light, the *Truth* is attained.   404-1

Common sense and a loving heart have made it possible for her to see the end of her cycle in the earth.

A Healer
[500]

... there is more required of those that are aware.
500-1

Healing was the dominant theme of three previous lives outlined for this young woman, whom we will call Virginia. It seems, therefore, that becoming a naturopath was a choice directly in line with her past experiences and inner promptings.
The reading begins with a discussion of the importance of experiences in mental dimensions between lives which the readings call "planetary sojourns." It states that astrological, numerological, signs and omens greatly influence Virginia's life. It goes on to suggest that she wear the Maltese cross and a stone of agate or amethyst. Later in the reading we see that the Maltese cross is related to a past life. These amulets are not to be depended upon as though they were good luck charms, rather their subtle vibratory influence would be helpful in increasing her efficiency in times of stress.

In giving the relationships that make for influences in the experience of this entity, we will find that from the unusual development in many environs that have been and have become accredited as active forces in the experience of the entity, no *one* may be said to be more influential than another. Yet the sojourns in other planetary environs make for periods when all of these influences may make for the greater urges within the mental being of the entity. Astrological, numerological, signs and omens—all have their part in the experiences in this entity's environ. And it would be found that in numbers the two and nine become the more often in the experience, as related to those conditions in activities when numbers deal with same, yet the "lucky number" for the entity would be thirty-two; and it would be very well if you ever bet on that horse or on that number—but don't bet, unless you're just playing! Yet these things of chance would oft enter the experience of the entity.

The soul's development or retardment depends upon whether individuals allow such influence to become active in their mental experience in relationships to the other conditions that exist in their lives.

As to the astrological aspects, as we find, these are of specific activity. The omen the body should ever wear on the person is a Maltese cross, or a stone of the agate or amethyst—for their vibrations are the better. But, as the body should comprehend in regard to all such influences, it is as to what the body does about same; not that it relies upon such, but knowing that such influences aid in increasing the ability or efficiency in the periods of exertion or activity, use them rather as stepping-stones and not those things upon which the activities in a mental and spiritual plane would be builded. They are step-stones rather than foundations, then, in the experience.

The following explanation of the astrological aspects credits Virginia's mental abilities to the influence of Mercury. The reading points out that the results of a life depend upon how the self reacts to what it knows and understands.

From Mercury we have the mental efficiency, the mental abilities of the entity; yet, as the entity has experienced and may experience in the application of those things influencing its life—or its use of life in this particular sojourn, the results depend upon how the self reacts to that it knows, understands or comprehends, rather than saying that it is true two and two would always be four. But if thought was an influence that one and four still made four, this would—because of the entity's activities upon same—become to the entity the established influence; yet the intelligent activity of the mental forces, the relations of things as to other things, the relations of various vibrations as to other vibrations, make only for those same laws in the numerological order. However, if the odor of two violets were added to the odor of two roses, while only four odors would be made, many more than four odors may be

82

discerned by the very essence of the basis of those in numerological influences that have produced same.

Hence the mental applications of the entity in the influences from Mercurian activity have made for abilities, particularly in the last two and a half years, in the activities of the body, that have been even to self not altogether comprehended. And when these influences from the sojourns in the environ are maintained with the sojourns in Jupiter and Venus and Mercury, in those associations in their influence as to make for the greater activity in the experiences of those who have sojourned within that environ, the entity may in the next two years find—then—the greatest period of efficiency, or the period of the greatest efficiency that the body may have during the sojourn in this experience.

After predicting that the next two years will bring a period of great opportunity the reading poses the question: Has fate or merit provided this period?

The natural question asked by the entity, then, would be: Is this the destined activity of the body, or is it merited through the influences that these planets have been in the sojourn about the earth or in that environ?

Such conditions are rather the result of merits, and as the entity applies the knowledge it has—as the knowledge of two and two making four, yet that two and two odors combined make the reactions such as may come from the sojourn in other influences—they may be used and applied, not abused; for the abuse of even privilege, the abuse even of love, the abuse of any of the virtues that are in the experience of every soul, brings turmoil, discontent, unharmonious influences; yet *used* in their relationships bring to each soul the knowledge of the love that is shed in the earth to the sons and daughters of men from a benevolent influence that we may call Creative Force. Or, would that all souls should know that God, the First Cause, the First Principle, would have those forces manifested in the experience of all that they may be one with Him through the love that has been patterned for all—as in the mount, as in thine own body, as in the body of Him that came into the experience that we through Him might know the Father, having the Advocate with the Father—or the knowledge, the consciousness, the awareness that He dwells within.

As to the applications, then, of those things that may shortly come to pass from the astrological influences in the experience of this entity, know that with the greater possibilities, the greater obligations assumed by those even that use that influence with the abilities, there is more required of those that are aware. Some, then, dare say that ignorance is bliss; yet to stumble in the darkness to become as the groper and the dependent one upon another influence. Yet the crying has ever been from the Father that each soul should stand upon its own feet and dare to call God its Father, its God, and claim the right to be one with Him, and not a groveler in the dust of the earth—or a groper.

The answer, then, is merit. The entity develops as it uses, not abuses the knowledge it has. This brings to each soul an understanding of the love from the Creative Force: partially stated, little is asked of a blind groper, but much is expected of one blessed with light.

Virginia is told that she may reach such an awareness that she need not choose to re-enter the earth should she decide to "develop on." The possibility is dependent upon what the soul does with the ability it has in hand. However, the reading indicates that ties of love may cause her to desire to return.

Hence in this experience may the entity come to know such an awareness that it need not choose to re-enter the earth, if it so desires to develop on; or if the ties become such that there would be those wishes or desires in the inner self to stand in stead of those that there had been created that love within, then again may it manifest in the desires of the experience. This is a possibility, dependent—of course—upon what the entity, the soul, does with that ability it has in hand.

Before the discussion of past lives the reading points out that Virginia's urge for physical activity, expressed in her chosen profession, comes from her accumulated past lives.

As to the appearances, then, that influence the entity in the present experience, in such ways and manners as to have brought certain definite urges—not so much of the mental as of the urge to activity in the physical reactions of the body, these—we will find—have been many, and in many varying experiences and activities; yet these, as we find, are those that make for the greater urge in the present activities of the entity.

Atlantis and Egypt

This pattern began in Egypt where she had worked in hospitals and cared for children. Basically she had lost in that experience through the misuse of spiritual influences. Nevertheless, a pattern was started.

Before this we find the entity in that land now known as the Egyptian, during those periods when there were those coming from the Atlantean land when there were the establishings of the relationships with other classes that entered in; for turmoils and strifes had been rampant in the land when the entity came, among the natives of Poseidia.

The entity assisted in the hospitals, and the aid in the care for the young; making for a dissension with the leader in this activity when the entity joined itself rather to those in Ibex and later established the activity for self in Abyssinia where the exile had been spent. Hence losing for itself, because the entity became the priestess in that land and brought many a rite or rote to those peoples that brought an influence that was the mis-use of the spiritual influences—through the rhythm of body, through the rhythm of incantations, through the movements that were brought by those influences; and thus retarded in that experience, in the name Istulo.

Egypt and Persia

Evidently she had another life in Egypt. The reading states that at a much later period she was among those going from Egypt to Persia to discover and share intellectual and spiritual knowledge. At that time great work in healing was taking place near what is known today as Shushtar, Arabia. She is said to have gained through that experience in spite of the fact that she caused much dissension. She was at that time some kind of physician. It is said that she prevented certain marriages because of the physical disorders of one or both parties. This was the same kind of work that she had separated herself from in her other Egyptian incarnation—a purification of the human body so as to be a vehicle for a soul to inhabit. The glorifying of the body was to reach its height much later in Greece. In that lifetime she had worked not only on ways to preserve the body but also on ways to preserve the truth being taught then. The latter was preserved in tablets and in symbols. The importance to her of the Maltese cross dates to this period.

Before this we find the entity in that land now known as the Arabian or Persian, during those places and peoples when there was the dissemination of those tenets and truths that had been gathered by a nomad people—yet that came to mean much to many peoples in many lands, and a city and a commercial center—in a manner—between the east and the west—then had grown up.

The entity was among those peoples that came up from the Egyptian land during that sojourn, and aided in establishing for their own peoples as well as those of the eastern lands the co-relationships where they might meet on the common ground for the understanding of their religious cults, educational factors—as they would be termed in the present day, that might bring into the experience of those in the various centers that which was being taught by that leader in the land.

Throughout the experience the entity gained, yet causing much turmoil; for the entity then prevented many of those associations in what would now be called wedded life, on account of the various characters of disorders in the bodies; and this brought dissension, yet those activities in the land that rose in its beauty later in the Grecian influences—not in that day, but the later day when beauty of body was almost worshiped—were begun by the entity in those sojourns in a hill city near what would now be called Shushtar, Arabia—or Persia. And there may be found in those tombs there, much that the entity accomplished in the way of making for the preservation of bodies and of those tenets in an unusual way and manner. These are in tablets, and—as indicated—the sign or symbol that should be worn may be found; because they *still* carry on them much of the symbols that would be written from the Maltese cross—as would be termed in the present, but then called the Yahama [?].

England and America

Virginia had been among the settlers in the lost colony on Roanoke Island, taken under the wings of Chief Powhatan at the time when the colonists were dying of starvation. Here she learned the medicinal value of herbs found in the forest and eased many kinds of suffering. She is said to have risen to prominence and to have been widely sought after by the Indians. In addition she sat in on a Five Nations pow wow and advised the Indians on how to better themselves and how to deal with the white men who came as settlers. "The ability to use influences of nature" learned in this period relates directly to her current profession of naturopath.

Before this we find the entity in this present land and among those peoples that were called natives of the land, with and among those of the household of one of the great chiefs of the land; yet the entity was born of those peoples that had journeyed to the land—and when there came the starvation to the peoples in Roanoke isle, when there were the changings, and when the great chief of that land went in search of the Friends that had been among the peoples. The entity then was named Virginia, yet—in those associations—the name was changed to Alahoi (A-O-I) [?] by the chief Powhatan. And in those environs the entity grew to become chief among those that aided in the application of the surrounding environs to aid in the ills and in the activities of the peoples, rather than the tom-toms or those influences that brought the activity of what was called the medicine man. The entity brought ease to many, aid to those that suffered with all characters of disorder or disturbance, and rose to one of power that was sought far and wide by a mighty peoples. And when there had been the activities in and among the chiefs of the five great nations, as they met in their pow wow within the Octagon [?], what is now known as the bank of the Ohio, the entity then acted as the counsel to those peoples as to how they might better themselves, even with their relationships to those peoples that later entered in to become the settlers of the land.

From the experiences (for it developed throughout) we find the activities in the present as of no strange lands, no strange places or peoples; and the ability to use those influences of nature in their proper relationships to those activities of individuals. Also the abilities within the entity to act in the capacity of the counsel between those where disturbances or disruptions may have been made in any character or nature. These were indeed developments for the entity, and harken to many of those that have come as mysteries of old; for to the entity much that had been given by those peoples from the sons of this fair land—especially where the sons of the Atlanteans had settled and later became the Mound Builders, when joined with the peoples that had crossed the Pacific—is innate in the entity. Hence mysteries, rites, rotes that pertain to strange peoples in strange places, to the entity find their answer in the self through the associations in that sojourn.

The feeling of "no strange lands, no strange places or peoples" is said to be a result of that life. Yet we notice that in each of the three lives given she had made her life in a country foreign to her place of birth. She had gone from Atlantis to Egypt, from Egypt to Persia, from England to America.

The reading ended with this advice:

In the present experience the entity finds self often confused by influences from without and from within, taking issue rather within self; and yet, as indicated from its experiences, if there is applied more of those tenets that were seen in the Arabian—and even in the appearance as Alahoi [?] in the Virginian land, as now called, there may come—in the application of self for bringing influences in the experience of others—that which will answer to the soul's desire to know itself to be at-one with that Spirit that is sought by every one as the *one* force in the life, in the experience, in the sojourns throughout the earth, or in that matter, for the expression of the Fatherhood in His beings.

Keep thine body, thine mind, thine soul, pure. Let no question be in thine inner self as to whether there is being accorded the *best* thou knowest in *thine* own environ. He requires nothing less, and nothing more.   500-1

An Engineer
[2504]

> . . . In each of those experiences, self-aggrandizement has never been a fault.   2504-4

Mr. Cayce's secretary, Gladys Davis, noted that the gentleman for whom this reading was given had had three physical readings prior to the life reading. The name in one of his incarnations suggests our pseudonym, Mr. Romuli. Planets symbolizing his innate mental tendencies are given as Jupiter, Venus, Mercury and Uranus. Present, therefore, are nobleness of spirit, largeness of vision, love of truth, capability of leading, and flexibility of mind.

Astrologically, we find the entity coming under the influence of Jupiter, Mercury, Venus, and Uranus. In the application of the will these influences are changed for weal or woe, as to be development *of* an entity through the earth's experience. In this entity, both latent and manifest, are seen many variations in experiences that have been both for development or retardment.

In the influences as are seen, and as are manifest:

One in the Jupitorian influence finds ennobleness, largeness of vision, bigness of purpose, and trueness of spirit.

In those as seen in Venus, of love for the truth, and the ability to apply those things that build toward self and toward the development of others—though in manners that at times are adverse to others' opinions; still, the love of those elements that bring for *trueness* in the experience *of* self is manifested by the entity *in* the life, and leads, influences, directs, many.

In those of the Mercurian, we find these have been, and will be used, in directions as would direct that as pertains to *ability* of understanding.

In those influences as appear in Uranus, to some the entity eccentric; to some the entity appears as one way at once and as siding with another side at another time. This rather the influence as would make for one being quick in mental vision, and quick in change of application when needs be to meet the needs of conditions as presented, rather than that of being untrue to the direction as is given by the entity's application of those things as elements in the experience of life.

One that influences, then, individuals.

The reading goes on to indicate that Mr. Romuli would have made an excellent politician, that he is much interested in machinery, engineering, and home building.

One that would have been a real politician; not politic in the manner of throwing away opinion without a purpose, but one that would be politic for the sake of individual, class, group and mass application of truth in the *experience* of those so served.

One that has the turn for mechanical appliances as related to *movements,* as have to do with machinery. These have been more of the *interest* than of application to same, though—as we will see—the entity *has* been, through the experience, a real engineer.

In those efforts of the entity in the present experience, these we find will and do lie in following the tenets of that as in nobleness of purpose, love of home, family, fireside, and in the young and old, applying self in the direction of building *up* same. Not merely making it a place, but *home*—as home means, in its real sense.

Egypt

In Egypt during the time of the Priest, Ra Ta, the entity had been among those who ministered to the people both mentally and physically. He had acted as an interpreter for immigrants from other lands. As a result, Mr. Romuli in his present life finds that reading in other languages comes easily to him.

In the one before this we find in that land now known as Egypt, in the period when divisions had arisen, and after the re-establishment of the peoples, and when the Priest was recalled, and the establishing of that school and that hospital, as would be termed now—or home. The entity one among those who ministered to the peoples in the manner of an aide to the understanding of the tenets as given, both by the Priest—as the theologian, and to the lecturer, as the one that would give lessons to the mental man, and from the physician—as would aid the physical man. The entity, then an interpreter for the peoples that came from foreign lands, for the peoples that were of the native land, for the people that were holders of the lands in that period. In the name Isdu. The entity gained through this experience, and in the present there is seen that influence wherein the reading of other tongues, or of other languages, are *easily* understood by the entity when the truth or the intent of that attempted is given.

Rome

As an early ruler of Rome, the entity had the name Romuli. That incarnation, in conjunction with the astrological influences, forms the basis of his interest in justice for all.

In the one before this we find in that land now known as the Roman. The entity then among those when the city was builded in the hills. The entity one of the rulers that came into

89

possession of the rule in the land, in the name Romuli. The entity gained through this experience, losing only in that of meting to others those punishments as had been meted to those the entity would conquer in building up the land. In the present experience, the influence rather that, that everyone in every plane should have justice dealt in the manner in which has been set it shall be meted for that offense. In this, it brings also rather that influence as over a stickler for law, law enforcement, law betterment, yet not *wholly* that as would be the lawyer or the judge—but rather as *one* of the many to apply same.

America

The most recent affecting life given is one as Benjmine, an assistant to an inventor "of the crafts that were propelled by machinery." The entity gained "in the application of self to the service of others." From that experience, Mr. Romuli carries into the present incarnation, an interest in new appliances and labor-saving devices.

In the appearances, and the effect these have in the present experience, as has been manifest, as is manifest:
In the one before this we find in that land that is the home of the present abode, but near a large body of water. The entity then an assistant to those who first made for the crafts that were propelled by machinery. In the name Benjmine. The entity gained through this experience in the application of self to the service of others, in that, that accomplished would bring comforts and enjoyments to those whom that created would serve. In the present experience, this has had an influence in the experience of the entity in being interested in the application of *new* appliances, as to labor-saving devices, as to those of circuitous routes in reaching the needs that would bring shorter cuts to the application of man's own abilities.

Looking at the present abilities, one common fault not found in this soul, according to the reading, is self-aggrandizement. In other words, Mr. Romuli cannot understand why anyone would put his own interests before those of his fellow man.

In the abilities of the entity, in the present:
These, as seen, lie in that of assisting, of directing, in aiding others, and in *this* the entity may excel—for, as is seen, in each of those experiences self-aggrandizement has never been a fault, and hard for the entity to understand an individual that is so warped in self as to set selfish interests before that of its fellow man. In keeping same, then, keep that in the tenets of that explained in Arrg [Og?], in the temple, or in the school called Arrg [Og?].

The reading ended with the statement that if he would continue living the same way, there would be no necessity to return to *this* earth, unless he should so *desire*. Again the intriguing combination of words—*if—this earth—desire.*

In the abilities as to the present experience, these may only be added—keeping in the way as has been seen, there will not be the necessity, unless so desired in the present, for the return to *this* earth, as an experience.   2504-4

A Dancer
[4500]

One who gives self in thought of others often in preference of self.   4500-1

There are many ways of giving self and bringing joy to others, and the past lives of this young woman illustrate some of them. We refer to her as Diana because once she was a priestess to the goddess of the same name. At other times a dancer or an entertainer, she consistently gave herself to the cause of making the lives of others happier and more harmonious.

In entering the earth's plane, we find the entity comes under the influence of many great ennobling influences, and is destined to lead, direct, and influence, the lives of many peoples; for the entity represents many influences as were sought after persecutions, yet worshiped in the hearts of many.

One coming often under the influence of Venus, Jupiter, Mercury, and benevolent influences of Saturn and of Neptune. Hence, we find one that is ever in the attitude of being hoped for, and bringing joy, peace, happiness, comfort, cheer, and love, in the lives of those whom the entity contacts.

One in whom love and reason are as the leading factors in the life.

One that, with the high ennobling influence in Jupiter, brings a great many honors of *natural* conditions to the experience of the entity, and tempered with the influences in Venus and Mercury brings peace and happiness to many; yet consternation in the lives of some for the welfare of the entity itself in spending of self, as it were, to gain the field of endeavor the entity finds self led to, on account of the innate feelings, or desire of entity to assist others in having a greater amount of cheer in their lives.

The entity would have made a *wonderful* nurse.

The entity would make a wonderful teacher in dramatic art, in expression, or as an interpreter of any of the legends of folk lore to individuals, groups as individuals, or as groups—for these are as the natural trend of the entity, and the entity is better pleased, satisfied—gains more from doing for others, than attempting even rewards of merit for self—see?

In the manifested influences in the present experience, irrespective of the will's force—for, as has been given, and as is seen, will's force is ever tempered by love and by judgment. Hence, without respect to will's force, these influences as have been given are the *natural* bend or trend.

In the application of will's force, we find as these:

One who gives self in thought of others often in preference of self.

One who, while gaining many positions of influence, is as the natural leader—yet never lording same over others; yet one very much given to consider position rather by merit than by chance—for to the entity, chance is as a small part in the life of any individual (yet the entity itself would be one who could almost break the bank of Monte Carlo—yet it would not be well for the entity to apply self in this direction, as will be seen by experiences in the earth's plane and the lessons gained from same). Hence will's force is manifested in such directions, and one never need be fearful of the abilities of the entity to direct, guard, or guide self in correct channels—unless overcome in the twenty-third (23rd) year by evil influences of ones influenced by Mars and Uranus; that is, the entity should ever beware of firearms, or those that are closely associated with same. While the sports are of a manner enticing to the entity, and in moderation are well for the physical conditions of body, beware of those that tend towards arms of destructive nature in any way or manner. In the Uranian is as of one that is an extremist, and would misconstrue purposely the intents of the entity itself in action. This, as we find, would occur during the months of—fifteenth (15th) of November to fifteenth (15th) of December.

In temperamental conditions, we find the entity even, and in the way of an example to those who would use self or self's gifts attained in a correct way and manner to bring joy or goodness in the lives of those who are to the entity as companions, or as friends.

One is impressed by the focus on the natural tendency toward leadership, and the attendant comment that in such positions she would not "lord it over others." It is a theme to be repeated. Not only was Diana told that she would make a wonderful nurse or a teacher of dramatic art, she was told that these abilities were largely a result of lives in the distant past.

Egypt

The earliest life given was one in Egypt, where Diana's involvement in temple worship through music and dance "brought joy and happiness to man."

In the one before this we find in that period when the laws and the church were of one, and made in that period in the Egyptian forces when church and state divided, as it were. The entity then among those who gave in the temple worship the song, the praise, and the ability of individual to give rhythm and the harmony of voice and body. Hence the urge as is seen to ever temper the truths as given or as manifested by entity by the early training of the church. In the abilities, then, did the entity surpass those about same, and many of the inner shrines will today, now, be found bearing the inscription of the entity in that period—Isssi. And the entity gained through that existence and experience, for the worshipfulness of the entity brought joy and happiness to man.

Greece

The appearance in Greece continued the theme of temple worship and helpfulness to others. There she was a priestess of Diana, and she gained until she started to compete with others and was overcome by envy. This experience is said to account for the fact that in her present life she would refrain from competitive acts and thus avoid arousing envy in others. This goes along with the statement that she could be dominant without being domineering.

In the one before this we find in that Grecian period when the people worshiped the Gods from the mount. The entity then of figure and of position as was of by the writer of the day, representing to that peoples Dian—and the life and experience of the entity was well pleasing to the forces as were manifest through that period, bringing to the ones in bondage much joy, much sought for release from the servitude of others. The entity gaining—until that period of oppression brought in the earthly experience that of the one influence that gave that of the seeking to supplant others, or envy—and the entity finds in the present experience that *not* of envy, but of the well-manifested influence to prevent the supplanting of those who would envy the entity in its (the entity's) own position.

France

In early France, the entity Diana was again in a position to influence others. As an entertainer and the idol of the court she endeared herself to many. Although the situation was fraught with temptation, she abused neither her place in the spotlight, nor the luxury with which she was surrounded. Again she "gave, gave, gave to others in word, in deed." Her talent for making scenes and lessons come alive is credited to that incarnation.

In the one before this we find in the period of the first kings in country now known as France, when the ruler was given to manifest through the play presented as entertainment for court and subjects. The entity then the idol, as it were, of the peoples and of the court, in the name then Briedlan, and the entity gained through that experience, in bringing joy, peace, happiness, to many, and in same brought to self that position of a satisfaction in a life well spent, even in luxury—though never abusing same, for the entity gave—gave—gave to others, in word, deed—and in the minds of many was the leading figure during those periods of this entity's sojourn. In the urge is seen that desire to express self in manifestations of word and act of the body. Hence the ability to teach, train, or to *read* in such way and manner as to bring the greater influence in the lives of the hearer.

Diana's incarnations were lives of harmony. As a worshipful entertainer guided by the Christ within, she thought of others and brought cheer and peace by setting an example even under tempting circumstances. She had attained much through correct use of her talents, yet she was admonished to "keep in the way that leads to the cross."

In the experiences then of the entity, and the abilities, as may be manifest in the present earth's experience, these lie in that of the teaching, the reader, or the interpreter of any of the lessons and truths as are given to the peoples through the voice, and through the rhythm and harmony of the body—and in same, the entity should ever temper same with that truth as is found and as manifested in Him to whom the entity has ever looked for the guidance and the directing of ways. In the harmony then of life does the entity find the manifestations of that in the holy of holies as is seen in the creative energy in the material or physical world. Keep—keep—in that way that leads to the cross, for in Him is the light, and the manifesting of that light through the entity's endeavors will bring the crowning joys of the entity to the point wherein no *earthly experience* will be necessary in the entity's development other than the present, for the entity is in that sphere of development surpassing many. Use aright, and all is well.

4500-1

94

A Wise Man
[256]

*... apply will's influence, by keeping an ideal—not
an idea—an ideal—before self ...*   256-1

A teacher of accounting when his reading was given, Mr.
Islac was daily steeped in numbers and mathematics. The story
emerging from his past lives shows that this expertise was but
a shadow of previous lives of deeper studies. The reading
encouraged him to study the mysticism of numbers and
astrology, and said emphatically in answer to his first question
that he should become the astrologer for the Association's
membership. That, however, was not to happen.

Early in the reading he was told that, by using his will to
build toward an ideal, he could reach the point where few, if
any, additional appearances would be necessary in the earth.

**In entering we find astrologically the entity coming under
the influence of Aquarius and Venus, Jupiter, Mercury, and
Neptune. Water will ever be a factor in this body's endeavors.
The body should ever live near large bodies of water. Be more
careful of those of high mountains or gorges, and of distant
places.**

**In entering, we find the influences that give to the entity
exceptional abilities in the present experience, in lines or
individual factors. These, kept in the manner toward which
the entity would apply will's influence, by keeping an ideal—
not an idea—an ideal—before self, will build for self that which
will carry the entity to where few, if any, appearances would
be necessary again in this mudane sphere.**

As the astrological influences are described, the aptitude for
mathematics is brought out. The personality that comes into
view is one of an idealistic man to whom money means little but
people mean much. Love rules his life in many respects
although outwardly he doesn't seem to be particularly
affectionate. It appears that the love he feels is more universal
than personal. Mr. Islac is strongly encouraged to study
numerology and astrology.

**In the abilities as come through the influences in Aquarius,
we find the entity could, or would, be able to apply self in
influencing those that had to do with mathematical
calculations, especially regarding aeronautics or boat
building. The entity may become an architect beyond compare,
provided these have to do with those elements that have to do
with water or air.**

Those influences in Jupiter and in Neptune bring for the

entity those desires of study, those desires of loneliness; yet the life filled with those conditions that have to do with people. People and things, *both,* interest the entity. The barter and sale interest little. Moneys mean little to the entity, save as for that to procure that necessary in the affairs of everyday life. Rather those of character, and those of that that builds for an individual as to being their worth, and their worth to the entity meaning their ability to aid in given direction, or in giving to individuals or groups that which will aid them in making life either easier or more profitable—whether for moneys or for pleasures, or for own development.

In the likes and dislikes for this entity, these are apparently contradictory—for affection or love *rules* the life in many respects, yet little affection is shown, except in some directions—yet the deeper affection, as friendships, and love of individuals and of things, are to the entity of the same nature—yet these, builded in a manner, are better in the application in the present experience. To the entity friendships are strong. Dislikes are also strong, but the actions in dislikes are rather as if they did not exist, or as if individuals or things did not exist. The entity then is, in a manner, *not* a fatalist, yet activities would tend to make one believe such were the innate beliefs of the entity. Rather the love of the whole, or of the oneness of all force, gives that portion in the life that brings those conditions which build.

In the mathematical end of developments may the entity gain much, especially in study that has to do with the mystic, and the mysticism of numbers. These to the entity may be made much worth while. The entity may aid self, aid others, in the study of not only astrology but astronomy, and numbers as associated with same; aiding individuals in that, through that, that may be builded from character, as related to individual development, and the entity may then find that which will, may become, in *this* individual application of truths, that as the astrologer then for same, through numbers. Not through astrology alone. Rather numbers, and the application of numbers and numerology in its *deeper* sense. These are the elements that interest the entity. These may be worked out with mathematical precision in *many* individuals, yet applied with that as may be attained from an individual's life appliance—that is, the application of the individual towards life itself, or towards the entity's application of life in its own individuality, these may aid much in the establishing of truths in these directions.

Egypt

The earliest incarnation given was in Egypt where he gained a great understanding of mathematics, geometry and astrology. He could easily understand Einstein's theory, he was told.

In the one before this we find in that land where divisions arose, or as may be called Egypt now, when there was the building of those that came to understand the teachings as were being propounded by the professors, the doctors, the lawyers, the artisans. The entity builded in that of setting up the first study of how that the square of the one equal in the square of the other, as related to numbers and the *positions* of numbers as related to the stars in the universe, and the relation of one to another. The entity will *easily* understand Einstein's theory. Few would!

Arabia

Scholars have long maintained that the three Magi were astrologers. Mr. Islac was told that he was the wise man who brought the frankincense. Here we see a pattern of continuation of studies begun earlier in Egypt and a profound understanding of the universal forces.

In the one before this we find the entity was among those who were of the Wise Men coming into Jerusalem and to Bethlehem when the Master came into the earth. The entity then in the name Ashtueil, coming in from the mountains of what is now known as Arabia and India. The entity gained through this period in pointing out that through the various forces as were added in the experiences of man with that creation of forces necessary to keep the balance in the universal forces, the earth must bring forth that that would make man's balance of force with the Creative Energy as one, and the Son of Man appeared. The entity brought frankincense and gave same to the Master at that period.

England

The third and last life given shows Mr. Islac as a monk in England at the time of the Crusades. Unable to journey to the Holy Land, he resented those who, he felt, were able to go and fight for the defense of an ideal.

These three lives show a pattern of scholarship, mysticism and dedication to an ideal. The implication of a number of solitary lives explains references in the astrological section to "the desires of study, the desires of loneliness" as well as "the love of the whole, or of the oneness of all force." In this life he did not marry until after he was forty.

In the one before this we find the entity was the monk in that rule when the peoples in now England set out for the Holy Land to defend the Cross against those inroads of the then surging crowds or hordes over the land. The entity remaining, yet following same and ever begrudging, as it were, those that were able in physical manner to carry forward that felt within self the defense of that ideal. In the name Islac. The entity changed same in the taking of the hood, to that of Adria. In this present experience, these of study—these of the stars—these of mystic numbers, places, conditions, are all absorbing to the entity. Rather apply same as to the relationships of numbers, mystic forces and symbols, to that of the creative energies as are given through Him that came as the ransom for many, making man one *with* the Creative Energy in the life, in the manner of showing forth to others that the pathway may be led in the direction where all may be one with that Energy. So, in numbers—so, in mystic forces—so, in the cycle of things— may *this* entity, applying same with the life as led by the Master, guide many—as aids in the physical, in material, in spiritual life.

The reading ends with the present time, and a repetition of the same theme:

In the abilities in the present experience, the entity gains and loses. Loses in the gratifying of selfish desires.

In the application of the present, still we find figures, numbers, and peoples' mental development, most interesting.

As to the abilities, then, and the application of same in the present—in the studies as are being made here, will the entity apply self in that direction, the entity may become that one that may aid much in having individuals understand numbers, mysticism of numbers; also in the relationships of *astrological* effects (without the application of will) in the lives of individuals.   256-1

This was not to happen, at least not in the way envisioned in the reading. Busy with school and a promotion that took him out of the classroom into an administrative position, he said in his letters to Mr. Cayce that he hoped to make time to study along the suggested lines, but there is no indication that he ever did so.

Eleven years after the reading he was dead. His sister wrote to Mr. Cayce saying that her brother's passing had been a terrible blow. She wrote:

"Only God knows why he had to leave us. I feel that perhaps he had God's work to do, and as he was not allowed to do it here, the higher forces removed him to where he could do it.

"His wife was up in the country at the time, and he was alone in the house. His mother-in-law called him on the phone at 8 A.M. and asked him to come over for some breakfast. That was on Wednesday, the 25th. He answered saying that as it was so late he'd go right along to school and get a bite on the way. The garage is attached to the house, and he was found there that night at 10:30—must have been lying there all day. The coroner said it was carbon monoxide poisoning. He had a flashlight burning in one hand and a wrench or something in the other—his hands were greasy, they said, and the motor was still running. The door from the house into the garage was open—but the doors opening into the driveway were closed. The garage was so small that there was just room on the sides of the car to let a person pass—but when he was found he was on his back and had a large lump on the back of his head. They said he got it when he fell.

"It was his wife's sister's husband who found him. From the very first I have had a feeling that someone might have done it. I may be wrong—but this morning his wife called me and said that they have not been able to find his wallet or his wrist watch.

"He looked beautiful in death. His hair had gotten pure white—and such nobility and peace I have never before looked on. The chapel of the undertaking establishment where he was buried from on Sunday was packed with former students and teachers from the school, and many friends—and all who ever knew him are grieved. My mother [403] has had great courage, but it is pitiful for her to have such a sorrow after all she has been through. I myself loved him more than my own life—and I know that you loved him, as he did you. There isn't anyone on earth who can tell us how he met death—I mean what the circumstances were. Is there any way in which we could get a reading on it?

"Two nights after he passed I was talking to him in a dream. At the time I didn't realize that he was gone, but he sat on the side of my bed and spoke very quietly with me. I didn't look up into his face, but as I looked sideways at his body it was clothed in a beautiful gown—sort of creamy with a shade of yellow and soft rose. I feel that the masters let me see him so that I would know he was all right, as I did grieve terribly for him. After that it wasn't so hard to bear. I feel that we (he and I) will do much work together in God's service. He couldn't have done it here; perhaps that is why I am left. However, if there is any possible way to find out whether his death was an accident, or whether someone did it, it would not bring him back I know but would lay the doubts that we have about the whole thing."

Edgar Cayce responded to the sister saying that if her departed brother wished to communicate that he would do so in a dream or a vision. The sister agreed:

"You are right—if [256] wants to communicate to us any of the details of his passing he will do so himself. However, I know him well enough to know that if he thought that another would be punished on his account he would keep it all to himself—and pray for them. His wallet was mailed back to his home with only the papers in it. His watch has not been found . . . They missed him at school that day but as he was promoted last year to a position where he did not teach any more—had his own work and office— he sometimes was away on school business, and they didn't think anything of it . . . it was not until 10:30 p.m. that his brother-in-law found him."

Later Mr. Cayce wrote to the sister:

"Last evening I had a very lovely experience with [256]. I was with him again on a visit in ____[Mass.]. (You possibly remember that several years ago [in 1930] I spent a day in ____ [Mass.] with [256]. We drove about the city, to the school and many places of interest.) Well, this morning we did that all over again. Then, when I was leaving him he thanked me for writing you. So I think I know just what you mean—about your worries, but you will have lots of help in many ways about all of them. He is happy and all is well."

Two months later the sister answered:

"I know [256] must have been very happy to see and talk with you again. I have had two experiences in Nov. while semi-conscious. [256] came twice and spoke with me. I realized in both that he had come back from the other side. The first time was while I was in the hospital and was a very trying ordeal for me, because, while I was talking with him he closed his eyes, bowed his head, and started to disintegrate before my eyes. The next time that part was spared me as I realized he didn't have very long to stay and so didn't try to say too much, so as to detain him. I remember that I said, '[256], you didn't want to go, did you?' And he said, 'No, I didn't.' May the peace of God be with him."

In June of the following year she wrote to Gladys Davis:

"Tell Mr. Cayce that I have spoken with our dear [256]. He is happy, and doing the spiritual work there that he could not do here. It is true that he was slugged and left to die in the garage, where the motor was running. He would not tell, or give, even a hint of who did it, asking only that I pray for them. (As I write this, he asks that I send his love and blessings to the dear ones whom we both know—remembering former years.) God, in His infinite wisdom and mercy is good to His children."

It may be necessary for this wise man to return to fulfill his ideal. Or perhaps by the way he forgave when his life abruptly ended, he was able to go on to other realms of service and study.

A Conqueror
[115]

> ... the conquering of self is truly greater than were
> one to conquer many worlds ...   115-1

This discerning soul has learned to exalt the Spirit and not the self. She entered under the influence of Venus, Uranus, Jupiter, and Mercury, but, says her reading, predictions based on these astrological urges would not match with the life she is living. Her will, it seems, is stronger than any mental or emotional urge.

In entering, we find the entity coming under the influence of Venus, Uranus, Jupiter, Mercury. In the astrological aspects, these would, in a manner, be contradictory to that as has been builded in the entity in the present experience. Also there will be seen variations in the application of the entity's experience in various other experiences in the earth's plane. So, in this instance, again we would find, astrologically, astronomically, or even in numerology, [these influences] would not coincide with the experiences of the entity, save as a general manner, or as may be termed—in common parlance—the variation as is exhibited in this entity's experience would prove a *rule* that may be made helpful; though, as has been seen, a *life* experience may be made *more* helpful for the entity.

The effects of the influencing planets on the personality are given—with the stipulation that the comments are general and results depend on the use of her *will*. She is described as one who loves and honors her fellow man; one with a mystical nature who uses her will to look ever upward; one with a broad outlook and strength of purpose; one with a good mind.

Then, disregarding the application of will's influence in the present experience, for a moment, we would find:

One naturely, or naturally, attuned to high emotions in life; whether this be of a secular nature or of the higher vibrations.

One that has ever been able to find beauty in *every* element, save when condemning self or condemning actions in another; yet ever feeling the vibrations have something to *do* with the individual; as would color or harmony of any nature; yet applying will and will's influence to these very same innate abilities (or preferably they should be called *qualities*) the entity then becomes able to harmonize same, so that in their synchronization there arises good from *whatever* experience a body, or an entity, may experience, will that entity but *use* same as a stepping-stone, rather than a stumbling block, or a fallen column.

In the experiences as have been had in the earth's plane, these alter or change much in the various experiences of the entity, so that there may be seen many variations, and at times even contradictory *evidences to* the body, to the body-entity, and same has at times become the rough hewn pathway that had led the entity on. Even in mental and physical anguish has the entity *developed* in the manner of application of the experience to self's *own* interest; not selfish in motive, not bigoted in act, not wayward in thought, but tempered and temperate in all things.

In the astrological urges—these are evidenced in the present experience, and these be the applications in the present experience of both the *innate* feeling or experience and the application of will, or self, *to* that experience.

In Venus—love for the fellow man; not as pity—rather as honoring the abilities of the individual in the direction as may be taken by that individual for the development of self as a whole toward others.

In Uranus is seen those of the occult and mystic nature, tending to either raise one's vision to a high degree or groveling in the slough of despondency. In will's lift up, look up, raise up, has ever been the entity's *innate* expression. *Will* has influenced the entity *much* in this direction, and in the hours of greatest despair has come the light that is ever available when a body-entity allows the divine—of which the soul is the spark, or portion—to enter in and make his abode there.

In Jupiter comes the bigness of purpose, the strength and might that either overcomes or is subdued by self, making in understanding, the ability to conquer in His name.

In Mercury the mental influences are abroad, either for the uplifting in the activities of the mental being, or turned into those of selfish natures.

In the application of self, this entity has gained the ability of discernment, and in the way of using the *little* in *hand* to gain the greater *understanding* of the whole.

After specifying that the entity can take much comfort from music, the reading recommends that she use music to raise her vibrations and further attune her soul. It might be possible that only her desire to help others would pull her back to another incarnation in the earth.

In music the entity finds *much* solace, much that bridges those disturbances—whether of the mental or of the spiritual forces. In same the attunement of self may be brought the nearest to the applications of the innate *forces* of self, and to the *entity* the strains of same—whether in that of the deep vibrations, of those that raise up and up—or those of the higher chords that bind—carry for the entity the *attunement* of self in the sphere or element, or *phase* of experience the entity seeks apace. Well were *this* developed to a more acuteness *in* this *present* experience, for the acumen of experience to the entity is gained *much* more in a manner that may become concrete ensamples of the attunement of a soul with the heavenly, or the happy, choir.

In color harmony—again—these often clash. In the harmony of strength or might the entity falters. This may be seen from the experiences of the entity. In a word, *much* has been made of the *present* experience, and it will lie within the own desire of the entity as to whether the return in earth's experience becomes necessary or not; for in Arcturus' forces, these become all magnified in will's force, and the conquering of self is truly greater than were one to conquer *many* worlds, and *is* conquering those of *our,* or of our *sun's* own attributes.

This case is another instance in which the emphasis was on development in the current life, in which the strength of the entity's will was stressed, and in which the effect of astrological urges was entirely subordinate, if not non-existent.

Atlantis

Five past lives were given. During the earliest one in Atlantis, this Conquerer of Self allowed her ideals to be subservient to her self-interest. She died in the first of the catastrophes that eventually obliterated the continent. Her soul was aware of the life's error and realized that divine knowledge should never be used selfishly.

In the one before this we find in the land known as Atlantis. The entity among those who held for the subserving of the ideals as to turning same into self-glory, self-satisfying; knowing much of the abilities of the peoples during the period of destruction, and destroyed *physically* with the first destruction that came to that peoples of *that* period; yet holding—holding—aloft, that the relationships of individuals' experience should be in accord with the divine, rather than using the divine for *selfish* motives; whether as fame, fortune, power, or *bodily* pleasure. In the name Asma.

In the abilities that the entity attains in the present, as to accord and the desires of the entity towards the people of the period, are still held aloof as worshipfulness of the power used for destructive rather than constructive forces.

Egypt

Appearing in Egypt during a time when invaders—among them Ra Ta, the Priest—took control of that land. The entity then was a member of the royal family of the native people. Having in the previous life worked for self-glory, she learned what it was like to have material glory forcibly removed. Although she became a recluse, she gained because of her work teaching the people chants, and she was responsible also for the inscribing of the oral tradition of the Book of the Dead. Her present responsiveness to music and color were attributed to that period. Stringed instruments could stir her soul memory.

In the one before this we find in that land when divisions arose, now known as Egyptian, and the entity then in the household of the ruler as was deposed when those of Arart came in from the north. The entity then that one who became the recluse and hermit in the halls of the house of worship, learning the peoples first of the *chant* for the dead; and the Book of the Dead were a portion of the *entity's* own inscribing. In the name Itasldhoia. In the experience the entity lost and gained, lost and gained. Gained in the latter experience, when there were harmonies set up and the chants were again heard in what later became tombs. In the present, much of that *innate* in the entity of music and color is a *portion* of the entity's inner being, and one from outside may play upon the chords of the entity's feeling in word, or song, or stringed instruments. Not the fanfare of the trumpet calls, but in *strings* much is felt.

India

Her lifetime in India was also during a time of strife. Previously in the court of a deposed king, she again was one of a conquered people. She had learned a lesson, for the reading says she was conquered in *body,* but not in *mind.* And in that life, married to one of her captors, she gave birth to Abraham. Thus she started the life as a virtual slave and ended up again in a position of authority.

In the one before this we find in that land now known as India. The entity then among those when there came the destruction of the peoples in the valleys by those who *would* make rule from the hills. The entity then among those that were *conquered* in body, but *not* in mind—and little by little the entity, through that experience brings to bear such influence, such a condition, as to bring the peoples who would become the rulers in accord with the mental and the spiritual *builders* of that land, and *of* the house came Abraham. Of the body came that leader, *that* people. In the name Terahe. *Not* the father, but the mother. In this present experience the entity finds history, travel, seeking of knowledge, study of stars, to the answer of a *something* not wholly understood; for in that period the great outdoors became the dwelling place of the entity, and much gain in position, power, abilities *to* aid, abilities to control, abilities to lead. The entity became the real *business* head of the then Chaldeans that arose later in the land.

Greece

One of gain and loss was her life in Greece. The gaining resulted from faith and service; the loss, from misuse of power. Once again she attained an exalted position, and with the curtain of memory closed over past lives, the power and temptation of fleshly fun—won! In that life her name was Xercia. Because as Xercia, she loved wine, dance and the spotlight, this Conqueror of Self is warned not to over-react or judge others who "express" themselves as she once did.

In the experience before this we find in that land now known as Greece, during that period when Xenophon carried on after the return from the eastern land. The entity then among those whom service was made and given by that ruler, or one in power. Gaining and losing through the experience. Gaining for the faith and service rendered many during the trials of that waiting. Losing in the mis-application of the power *gained* by being put in an exalted position. Many were the experiences for the entity followed *then* in the aggrandizing of *bodily* or *physical* desires, and the dance—the wine cup and revelry, in the desire for plaudit for plaudit sake, sought by the entity. In the present, these—we find some come among those tempting; yet be not hard upon those who seek in such manners to find expressions of themselves, for they know *not* what they do. In the name Xercia.

France

This time she served in the court of the exiled King of England, Charles II. She gained. This Conqueror of Self found in the exiled court a replay of the debauchery she had revelled in as Xercia, and yet she overcame and remained true to her ideal. She must have suffered as she resisted falling back into the old patterns. She learned to care for others while not participating in their self-dissipation. Charles II's antagonist at this time was Oliver Cromwell—Xenophon.

In the experiences in the earth's plane:
In the one before this we find not so great a way off for in the period when that dethroned monarch [Charles II of England?] ruled in France. The entity then an attendant, and an aide to, the offspring *of* those that suffered physically, and gained—even through the suffering. The fear of power, of might, without the divine influence of its rule, becomes *innate* in the entity from that which the entity suffered during that period. In the name Maithae.

She learned the lessons well. What she failed at in one life, she repeated and succeeded at in the next.

In the present, the abilities lie in the *innate* forces as the teacher, the guider, towards attuning self in harmony with the divine from within, and *harmonizing* self in color.

And as the reading presents this promise:

...*much* has been made of the *present* experience, and it will lie within the own desire of the entity as to whether the return in earth's experience becomes necessary or not... 115-1

Deftly has this soul plotted and made corrections in her course. A strong interest to manifest her best concept of how a person may serve others has opened the way for the greatest of earthly attainments—conquest of the self.

Chapter Four
NO NEED TO RETURN

If ye lay bound upon the wheel of change,
   And no way were of breaking from the chain,
The Heart of boundless Being is a curse,
   The Soul of Things fell Pain.

Ye are not bound! the Soul of Things is sweet,
   The Heart of Being is celestial rest;
Stronger than woe is will: that which was Good
   Doth pass to Better—Best.

          From *The Light of Asia*
           Edwin Arnold

    A variety of patterns emerges from the life readings of these eighteen people who were told that they might have the choice of not returning to the earth. Were they all saints? By no means. Their readings show them to be struggling with an assortment of problems. Frequently mentioned were lessons of patience, tolerance, and occasionally self-pity still to be mastered. Had all of these people's past lives been consistently on the plus side? Not at all. The readings indicate that in certain incarnations they had gained and in others they had lost. Mrs. Xercia (115) lost when she misused power and put selfish pleasure first. Virginia (500) who had a number of lives involving healing had lost when she misused spiritual influences and again when she had caused dissension. Mrs. Suthers, Nero's playmate, had been cruelly materialistic. Several, such as the lady described in A Christian Moslem (2112), lost because of holding grudges.

    Career patterns brought from life to life are shown in a number of these readings. In the cases of the architect (322) and the engineer (2504) it was involvement with government. Both the naturopath (500) and the psychiatrist (444) had had past lives devoted to medicine or some form of healing. The dancer (4500) had past incarnations predominantly as an entertainer. The mathematics teacher (256), who had been one of the Wise Men, showed a pattern of study of astrology and higher mathematics.

Counseling was said to have been an innate ability of the motherly Hannah (404), the peacemaker (1143), the counselor (2903), and Martha (500), who became the leader of the Glad Helpers Prayer Group. Although these people were not pursuing the profession of counseling, patterns from past lives would enable them to be of help to others as the need arose.

Other patterns have to do with the times when the individuals incarnated. There are a number of instances where past incarnations occurred during times of division, religious or political. These include the Christian Moslem (2112), the spinster Ella, the favorite (569), the peacemaker (1143), and the priestess (987). The time the readings were given was from the late 1920s to the early 1940s. During their present life they had already seen the world torn apart by one great war and another was on its way.

In Appendix B a chart is presented to facilitate comparisons of the biographical data, astrological influences and locales of past incarnations. It will be noted that certain periods are often repeated. Almost all had lives in Atlantis and Egypt; many appeared in the Holy Land and in colonial America. According to the Cayce readings it is usual for groups of souls to incarnate together. Ties of love and mutual concern or purpose bind us together.

The planets influencing the individual's mental nature in almost every case included Venus, Mercury and Jupiter. Very simply, the combination describes a loving person with a broad universal outlook. In one case, that of the Fiddler's Friend (5366), astrological influences were withheld. The reading for the Christian Moslem (2112) states that the person had changed completely from the indications of her astrological aspects, stressing that the use of the will could always alter those influences. Also, there are statements in the readings for a priestess (987) and for Mrs. Xercia (115) that, although astrological urges are present, they are relatively insignificant.

The eighteen people who had these readings came to Edgar Cayce from all over the country during the span of years between 1924 and 1944. Their educational and social backgrounds varied greatly, as did their choice of occupations. Their past lives were as highly individual as their present ones, but a common characteristic, or soul quality, emerges from a comparison of these readings in the very frequent appearance of a statement which is made in a variety of ways:

... the entity has in the most of its sojourns from the earth *given—given—given* of self ...   1143-2

... always giving, giving, giving, more than ever receiving.
569-6

One who gives self in thought of others often in preference to self.
4500-1

One, then, that gives much more to the development of others in every plane.
2903-1

... in each of those experiences self-aggrandizement has never been a fault, and hard for the entity to understand an individual that is so warped in self as to set selfish interests before that of its fellow man.
2504-4

Selfishness is not a portion of the entity's own being ...
987-2

... and the conquering of self is truly greater than were one to conquer *many* worlds ...
115-1

Then only as an individual gives itself in service does it become aware. For as the divine love has manifested, does become manifested, that alone ye have given away do ye possess. That *alone* is the manner in which the growth, the awareness, the consciousness grows to be.
1472-1

... in those experiences when self lost self—as it were—in that it gave to others, in the character of conditions that made for the losing of self in service to others, developments came to the entity ...
444-1

... for it may be said thou hast truly shown that thou preferest thy brother to thine own gratification!
322-2

... it is not what a mind *knows* but what the mind applies or does about that it knows, that makes for soul, mental or material advancements.
444-1

Although these people are outwardly quite different from each other in their present lives, they have in common a willingness to put selfish interests aside for service to their fellow man. These readings are not the only ones that stress service and the Biblical admonition that we only possess what we give away. Many references reiterate that service to others is the highest service to God, but this particular group of readings seems to demonstrate that until we can actually put it into practice and make it a soul quality, we probably won't be in a position to choose whether or not we want to return to the earth. Other readings in the group from which no specific quotes are taken often show a pattern of service in past lives (e.g., 1741).

In no instance did the readings say that the present life was the *last* one for the individual. The will of each person determines how his or her life will actually unfold. But the readings offer advice and encouragement, and they outlined how a person might truly reach the position of having a real choice about returning to earth.

Hold to those things that make for this ability to be tolerant, even with those that despitefully use thee. For it engenders strife to hold animosities.   1143-2

. . . there is the necessity for the entity to learn a little more of patience . . . not with others but the more with self. For as He gave, it is in patience that ye become aware of thy soul!

So in its associations with others the entity needs to forget those things that have made for hardships, that have made for misunderstandings in relationships as one to another—whether with individuals or with groups; though the entity may find oft that it requires that self turn within, that the consciousness of His Presence abiding may direct. Thus there may be brought peace and patience, as an *active* force; not as a passive influence in the experience of self but as an *active* influence!   987-2

For the entity has come a long way, and oft grows weary with the burdens not only that become a part of self's experience but that apparently are unburdened . . . upon the entity, in its dealings with those about self . . .

For He hath indeed given His angel charge concerning thee, and He will bear thee up if ye will faint not but hold to that purpose whereunto thou hast purposed in thy tabernacle in the present.

For know that His temple in thee is *holy;* and thy body-mind is indeed the temple of the living God . . .

. . . it is ever the Now and what the entity or soul may do *about* the consciousness or awareness that makes for those influences which are to be.   1472-1

. . . there is more required of those that are aware. Some, then, dare say that ignorance is bliss; yet to stumble in the darkness is to become as the groper and the dependent one upon another influence. Yet the crying has ever been from the Father that each soul should stand upon its own feet and dare to call God its Father, its God, and claim the right to be one with Him, and not a groveler in the dust of the earth—or a groper.   500-1

... *God* gives the increase. Be not in that position of one that frets about things, conditions, or peoples not *doing* as *you* would have them do! You may only be the channel through which the reflection of His love may be made manifest, for *God* works in His *own* way, own manner, and fretting self only brings those of discouragement, disillusions, as to those things that *He* would bring to pass.

Speak gently, speak kindly to those who falter. Ye know not *their* own temptation, not the littleness of their understanding. Judge not as to this or that activity of another; rather pray that the light may shine even in *their* lives as it *has* in thine. These are the manners in which the sons and daughters of men may *know* His way. In this mundane sphere there comes to all that period when doubts and fears arise, even to doubting thine *own* self. These may *easily* be cast aside by knowing that He is *in* His holy temple and *all* is well.

2112-1

Reflected in these readings is the necessity for adherence to the highest of ideals. In the case of the housewife (404) who was told that she was like a loving mother to everybody it was said that in her life in Egypt she had held true to "the ideals of an idealist." Many people in the period of the Priest's banishment carry scars on their personalities from the bitterness they felt at that time, but in keeping with her ideal, she avoided these scars by not holding a grudge.

The architect (322) was told:

... there have been opportunities where the entity could have acted for selfish motives without being questioned by those in authority, yet for self's own high ideals the entity has rather *stood* the test; and greater will be the crown for the soul!

322-2

Ideals carried over from life to life were apparent in "the golden cord" said to run through all the experiences of case (987). Another example was (2112) who in one life heard and accepted the teachings of Jesus, and held fast to those same ideals in a later life as a Moslem. The lady who had been a playmate of Nero was told that her only true hope was to "hold to that ideal of those whom it once scoffed at because of the pleasure materially brought in associations with those who did the persecuting." (5366-1)

For a more detailed look at the ideals from the Cayce readings' viewpoint, please see Appendix C. In that extract the statement is made that the purpose of an incarnation is to choose an ideal. How to choose it and what it should be is clearly presented there.

Each reference to the fact that an individual might not need to reincarnate again is a little bit different. Some start with strong encouragement to continue to hold the same high ideal by which they have been living.

... keep in that same way as has been set in self, in purpose and in manner, for through the own efforts in self there need not be the necessity in returning to earth's plane, for as is set, and if kept, these would develop into the higher spiritual realms, and then keep self in that way that leads to life everlasting, for in Him whom thou hast put thy trust is Life, for He is the Way, the Truth, the Light. In Him there is no guile.
569-6

Keep—keep—in that way that leads to the cross, for in Him is the light, and the manifesting of that light through the entity's endeavors will bring the crowning joys of the entity to the point wherein no *earthly experience* will be necessary in the entity's development other than the present, for the entity is in that sphere of development surpassing many. Use aright, and all is well.
4500-1

And, if the entity will apply self in those forces that make for the creating within self and those whom the entity may contact day by day, ideals that are of the standards making for Creative influences in the mind, the soul and the physical influences, through same may the entity gain and develop in this experience to those influences where only through the desire may it be necessary for the entity to enter earth's environs again.
Then, present self to those influences that make for Creative activities in such a manner that self may never fear to meet that it has spoken in word or thought; for each soul meets that it has meted, with those measures with which it has meted out.
444-1

... keeping in the way as has been seen, there will not be the necessity, unless so desired in the present for the return to *this* earth, as an experience.
2504-4

In entering, we find the influences that give to the entity exceptional abilities in the present experience, in lines or individual factors. These, kept in the manner toward which the entity would apply will's influence, by keeping an *ideal*—not an idea—an *ideal*—before self, will build for self that which will carry the entity to where few, if any, appearances would be necessary again in this mundane sphere.
256-1

The next excerpt, while not mentioning ideals or purposes, seems to suggest that the lady's current position as a governess was a perfect one in which to work on the ideal of service.

In the abilities of the entity in the present, as given, these may be made to excel—and the entity may so apply those tenets as have been set before self, in its ministration to those that are about the entity, that no return would be necessary in this experience or plane; for in Him is the light, and the light came among men, showing men the way to find that consciousness in self—for the kingdom is of within, and when self is made one with those forces there may be the accord as is necessary for "Come up higher. Being faithful over a few things, I will make thee ruler over many."   1741-1

Often when the statement about not being reborn into the earth appears early in the reading, it contains some observation as to why the person was thus singled out. Sometimes it is credited to a series of past lives, sometimes to the present life, and occasionally a specific trait is mentioned.

This entity may, with the keeping of those developments, make its peace in such a manner as for there to be few or none of the turmoils of the earth in its experience again.   1143-2

Quite an enviable position, may it be said, that the entity occupies; in the matter of truth, veracity, clean *living,* that the entity has made in this experience! and there will be little need, unless desired, for a return to this earth's experience.
For, there may be those cleansings that will make for, "Come thou and enjoy rather the glory of thy Lord, for it may be said thou hast truly shown that thou preferest thy brother to thine own gratification!"   322-2

. . . that may be said of *this* entity as of few we find through this experience—that may be builded in the present that will not require the entering into the earth's experience again; for much has been builded through the experiences in the earth's plane, and the sojourns have been those that have added to that, that to those who have come under the influence *of* the entity will—at *some* period in *their* experience—have been glad to have known the entity.
As has been seen, as has been given, in the present there may be attained that which will not require the entering into the earth's experience, but rather as the journeying on to those of the higher realms in which the entity may express or manifest self in that as has been gained.   404-1

When comparing these extracts, we see that the underlying key is the *will:* "unless desired" (322), "applying the will's influence to an ideal" (256), "only through desire" (444), "unless so desired" (2504), "use aright" (4500). Even the stress on keeping in the way that has been set implies the need to use the will. Other readings in the group are even more specific. One woman (2112) was told that she had exercised her will in such a manner that in the past three or four years she had made a wonderful development.

... the entity has set self aright. As to that it may attain lies only with self, for kept—and keeping the faith—never would it be necessary for the entity to enter into *this* vale, but rather to bask or journey through the presence of the faithful! 2112-1

One who may, with the present will forces, make self unnecessary for return in earth's spheres ...
Then keep in that way wherein He who gives the good and perfect gifts may be made manifest before men, knowing that unto Him all honor is due.   2903-1

A golden cord runs through the astrological, the numerological and the earth's experiences of this entity. The entity may complete its earth's experience in the present, if it so chooses.   987-2

... the *spiritual* life *of* the entity is such as to have *builded* for a development in this *present* plane to such an extent—that is, the *desire* such, and kept in present attunement—the earth need hold no cares for the entity in or after this experience.
                                                             560-1

Keep in that way that the development of the soul may be such as not necessary for the return, unless the entity so desires. Then it may bring to itself those conditions in its own mental forces through which the soul gains its development.
                                                             4353-4

The next selection emphasizes how ties of love may keep drawing one back into earthly incarnation, and keep one from developing on.

Hence in this experience may the entity come to know such an awareness that it need not choose to re-enter the earth, if it so desires to develop on; or if the ties become such that there would be those wishes or desires in the inner self to stand in stead of those that there had been created that love within, then again may it manifest in the desires of the experience. This is a possibility, dependent—of course—upon what the entity, the soul, does with that ability it has in hand.   500-1

The excerpt from the life reading of the woman who strung along with Nero adds some interesting dimensions to the idea of not reincarnating. It states specifically that perfection has not been reached.

114

This entity was among those with that one who persecuted the church so thoroughly and fiddled while Rome burned. That's the reason this entity in the body has been disfigured by structural conditions. Yet may this entity be set apart. For through its experiences in the earth, it has advanced from a low degree to that which may not even necessitate a reincarnation in the earth. Not that it has reached perfection but there are realms for instruction if the entity will hold to that ideal of those whom it once scoffed at because of the pleasure materially brought in associations with those who did the persecuting.   5366-1

This causes us to look at the other cases in another light. The implication has been that for some reincarnation is a certainty and for others, a certain amount of development makes possible a choice. Let us not jump to the conclusion that those souls who choose not to return are therefore ready to be one with the Father. "There are other realms for instruction" state the readings. Look at the subtle nuances in the phrases that described an entity's not having to return to *"this* earth," *"this* vale," *"this* mundane sphere." Perhaps choosing not to reincarnate into this earth is simply a step like graduation from a school, giving the soul further opportunities to make its will one with the Father's.

The next excerpt contains the only mention of Arcturus in these selections. Arcturus has been described in the Cayce readings as the exit point from this solar system (900-25).

Arcturus is that which may be called the center of this universe, through which individuals pass and at which period there comes the choice of the individual as to whether it is to return to complete there—that is, in this planetary system, our sun, the earth sun and its planetary system ... or to pass on to others ...   5749-14

In a word, *much* has been made of the *present* experience, and it will lie within the own desire of the entity as to whether the return in earth's experience becomes necessary or not; for in Arcturus' forces, these become all magnified in will's force, and the conquering of self is truly greater than were one to conquer *many* worlds, and *is* conquering those of *our,* or of our *sun's* attributes.   115-1

Earlier we considered the necessity of souls reincarnating—for their own growth and development—under the Wheel of the Law. The following extract illustrates another reason for an incarnation.

If there is kept that purpose in self, there is little need for a

**return; save as one that may lead the way to those that are still
in darkness.** 1472-1

Edgar Cayce was told in one of his life readings that he had
after his attainments in a pre-historic Egyptian life been
offered the choice of leaving this solar system via Arcturus. He
had chosen instead to return to the earth, which he did as the
great leader, named Uhjltd, in Persia. Although that life was
one of accomplishment, his life readings indicated that at the
end of it, his resentment toward the Greeks for destroying what
he had built forced him to return. In the next life he was a
Trojan who fought the Greeks.

The time will come when each of us shall have the choice of
returning to earth or developing further elsewhere. A return to
earth does not always mean attachment to materiality. It may
be that we, too, would choose to return to help others. In so
doing, we would be taking a chance of getting caught once more
in another cycle of return engagements.

A study of the cases indexed *Reincarnation: Unnecessary*
highlights for us the importance of service to others. In such a
way may we bring ourselves to the point where we will
determine to develop on in other localities besides the earth. If
we wish to develop through the limits of the earth plane and
progress along the line that was intended when we were
created, we certainly can learn from the examples shown in
these cases.

**Service to others is the greatest service to the Creator. The
desire to seek the greater forces will gradually bring, draw,
make, accomplish the desired end in the same manner as
pennies accumulated finally reach to the desired amount for
any purchase. Apply all rules pertaining to life to that.**
2725-1

What is the deciding factor? Nothing is external to us.
Nothing for which we need plead or bargain. Nothing that can
be set before us in our horoscopes. The deciding factor is our
own will. These eighteen people were told that they were
approaching this momentous crossroads because they had
used their wills. The same crossroads awaits each of us. And
the same method for getting there—will's ability to hold to the
ideal—resides in each of us.

**The astrological and the material sojourns then are urges.
These do not go beyond the will, that is the birthright of each
soul that it, the entity, may choose within itself that which is to
be the guiding influence in the experience.** 286-1

We need to use our birthright of will to control our thoughts as well as our actions, for "as a man thinketh in his heart, so is he."

For if the Mind dwells upon the spiritual things, then it follows that it becomes what it has dwelt upon, what it has lived upon, what it has made itself a portion of. But if the Mind dwells upon self-indulgences, self-aggrandizement, self-exaltation, selfishness in any of its forms, in any of its variations, then it has set itself at variance to that First Cause; and we have that entered in as from the beginning, that of making the will—through the Mind—at variance to Creative Forces before it has come into matter, into the movements in matter that we know as physical, material, as those things that are of the earth-earthy.   262-78

There is today set before thee good and evil, life and death—choose thou. The will then is the factor in the experience in material sojourns that makes for weal or woe, according to the influences chosen.

Hence the ideal in every phase of human experience and endeavor, as well as in the spiritual and mental, is used or abused by an entity in that choice.   843-9

And man, through the will, makes for his development or retardment through what he does about that he sees manifested in the material world.   262-56

Will is the birthright of the soul, and in the material plane of earth, it is exercised by the choices we make. No urge or power is stronger than our will. Only we determine whether we shall use that will to grow closer to the Creator or to put more barriers between Him and us.

"He who lacketh discrimination, whose mind is unsteady and whose heart is impure, never reacheth the goal, but puts more barriers between Him and us.

"He who lacketh discrimination, whose mind is unsteady and whose heart is impure, never reacheth the goal, but is born again and again.

"But he who hath discrimination, whose mind is steady and whose heart is pure, reacheth the goal, and having reached it is born no more."
                    Katha Upanishad

"As a man's desire is, so is his destiny. For as his desire is, so is his will; and as his will is, so is his deed; as his deed is, so is his reward, whether good or bad…"   *Brihadarayaka Upanishad*

How shall we apply our wills? The readings had this to say:

Just living those that are the fruits of the spirit: namely, peace, harmony, long-suffering, brotherly love, patience. These if ye show them forth in thy life, in thy dealings with thy fellow man, grow to be what? Truth! In Truth ye are free— from what? *Earthly* toil, *earthly* cares!

These then are not just axioms, not just sayings, but living truths! 987-4

The question was asked of Mr. Cayce, "Will it be necessary to re-enter the earth plane?" The answer was: "So live, so act, in the present that it will *not* be necessary." (295-2)

Q-4. Can I finish my purpose in this incarnation so that I will not need to return to the earth?
A-4. As may any; if they will but put *off* the old and on the new that is in Him; becoming aware of that I AM conscience within self that becomes one with Him. Yes.
Q-5. And how long will I have to do this?
A-5. How long will you require? 1037-1

Like the Prodigal Son we squander our birthright and wander far from our true home. At any time we can choose to start the homeward journey, encouraged that the reunion is ever possible. To finish our purpose and not return to the earth, we need to decide to put off the old and put on the new that is in Him.

How long will we require?

APPENDICES

APPENDIX A

There is one other reading indexed under *Reincarnation: Unnecessary* which is completely different from the preceding eighteen cases. They were all life readings and this is a physical reading. The boy for whom it was given was an abnormal child. The aunt who requested the reading wrote: "He's lived with me since the death of his mother. He can't ask for a reading and never will unless there's a change. He's been afflicted since birth." This reading says nothing about his possibly having a choice in returning. It says rather that he may be assisted. It states this life might make it possible for the soul to "build *towards* that point [from] which every soul and spirit force takes its flight"—Arcturus. The reading also suggests that the boy's physical and mental condition is karmic.

This Psychic Reading given by Edgar Cayce at Phillips Hotel, Room 115, Dayton, Ohio, this 25th day of January, 1924, in accordance with request made by [4502]'s aunt . . . *Present:* Edgar Cayce; Linden Shroyer, Conductor; Gladys Davis, Steno.

READING

Now in this body we will find those conditions that would be an interesting study psychologically, pathologically or biologically. From the psycho-analytical standpoint, we find manifestations in this present personage of that condition studied from hereditary standpoints, yet with the psycho-analytical forces we find the deeper forces producing conditions in physical [more] than from hereditary standpoint only, though this inertia had much to do with the present condition as manifested in the system.

This body, in the physical, may be assisted, yet never given the full perfect control of all of the portions of the system; yet the soul and spirit force will find in this entity that with the developing in self and in others that there will build to the developing upon this plane towards that point [from] which every soul and spirit force takes its flight, and to which purpose all individual entities are entered into the earth plane.

In the physical, we find that lack of coordination in the system that allows the physical to become a taxation to soul and spirit entity, and in this burdens even the higher elements of the physical forces, this produced physically from inertia, and (that is prenatal inertia) from the condition as the soul forces contracted through relativity of forces to the conditions surrounded before the body became a physical being.

In the action then of the physical in system to be overcome has to do with the nerve forces as connect between the cerebro-spinal sympathetic and the coordinating forces of the perineurial and hypogastric with the brain and the nerve systems.

Then, to give the best forces that will give some relief to this body, we would apply those conditions as are found in this: To two gallons of rain water, we would add:

½ lb. plain charcoal
½ lb. heavy sea salt
1½ lbs. copper sulphate
2 ozs. sulphuric acid C.P.
10 drams of common zinc

Preferably, this would be placed in a glass container. In this solution there would also be placed a one-pound opaque container of iodine. This whole solution then would be charged to heavy copper plates being placed in solution charged with the low battery charging formation until the solution will give off at least five and one half ohms in discharge.

To the positive pole there would be attached a heavy plate (nickel) which would be attached at the umbilicus. The plate should be large enough to cover the whole center surrounding this portion of the body.

The negative pole, with wire and smaller plate, would be attached at the first cervical.

This should be done for at least one hour each evening. When the solution has gone below the discharge of one and one-half ohms, then recharge the battery formation. They are connected by small wires to the plates that are attached to the body.

This should be kept for at least six to eight months. After the third or fourth charge, the massage over the whole system to carry the nerve ends through the system that make connection in those centers as governed from the pneumogastric, hypogastric, ilium, first and second cervical, and of the cardiac and the ilium plexuses. All of those should be massaged, so as to bring through to the whole circulation, and the gentle train of the mind should be with the treatments as given in the battery. Gradually control the mental forces, as will be shown in simple manifestations at first, and build into the system the desire of physical forces to be of assistance in developing in the present plane. Do that.

Care, persistence and attention must be given at all times. It is worth the price to any that would accomplish these. See that they are thoroughly carried forth, for in this we will see the manifestations of that injunction "As ye would that men should do unto you, do ye even so to them."

4502-1

APPENDIX B

READING NUMBER	YEAR READING GIVEN	SEX AGE VOCATION	BIRTH-DATE	PLACE OF BIRTH	PLANETS	PAST LIVES
115-1	1930	F., 53 Housewife	Oct. 7, 1876	Forest Grove, N.C.	Venus Uranus Jupiter Mercury	France Greece India Egypt Atlantis
569-6	1925	F., 45 Housekeeper	May 6, 1880	Mascoutah, Ill.	Jupiter Venus Mercury & Uranus in distance	France Persia Egypt
987-2	1935	F., 47 Housewife	Dec. 27, 1887	Northville, Mich.	Jupiter (ruling) Venus Uranus	New England (Salem) Persia Holy Land (Bible, Old Testament) Egypt
1143-2	1936	F., 48 Secretary	July 12, 1887	Leannighen Spa, England	Jupiter Venus Uranus	England Persia (time of Nehemiah) Egypt

READING NUMBER	YEAR READING GIVEN	SEX AGE VOCATION	BIRTH-DATE	PLACE OF BIRTH	PLANETS	PAST LIVES
1472-1	1937	F., 57 Writer, Radio-Broadcaster	May 5, 1880	Bowling Green, Va.	Jupiter Mars Venus Uranus Neptune	America (from England to Virginia) Palestine Egypt
1741-1	1930	F., 42 Governess	Feb. 3, 1888	Sargans, Switzerland	Uranus Venus Jupiter Mercury	Atlantis Egypt Lycaonia (Asia Minor)
2112-1	1931	F., 58 Apt. Manager	April 29, 1873	Norfolk, Va.	(Risen above astrological urges) Mercury Venus	New England (Salem) Moslem in Holy Land (Crusades) Holy Land—Jesus Egypt—division
2504-4	1929	M., 63 Real Estate	April 1, 1866	Waterford, Va.	Jupiter Mercury Venus Uranus	America Rome Egypt
2903-1	1925	M., 58 Life Insurance Repr.	Jan. 2, 1867	Hopkinsville, Ky.	Jupiter Mercury Mars	England Greece Egypt Peru (after Atlantis)

READING NUMBER	YEAR READING GIVEN	SEX AGE VOCATION	BIRTH-DATE	PLACE OF BIRTH	PLANETS	PAST LIVES
4353-4	1924	F., 20 Actress	Dec. 20, 1904	Ironton, Ohio	Venus Mercury Uranus Arcturus Variations in Sun, Mars and Jupiter	France Greece Persia Atlantis
4500-1	1927	F., 20	May 27, 1906	Peters, Fla.	Venus Jupiter Mercury	France Greece Egypt
5366-1	1944	F., 53	Oct. 31, 1890	A farm in Ohio	(Withheld) inconse-quential?	America Rome—Nero Promised Land Egypt
256-1	1929	M., 32 Accounting Teacher	Jan. 10, 1897	Boston, Mass.	Aquarius Venus Jupiter Mercury Neptune	England Persia Egypt
322-2	1933	M., 58 Architect	Oct. 25, 1874	Stapleton, Staten Island, N.Y.	Mercury Saturn Jupiter Mars	America Gadara, Samaria(?) Egypt

READING NUMBER	YEAR READING GIVEN	SEX AGE VOCATION	BIRTH-DATE	PLACE OF BIRTH	PLANETS	PAST LIVES
404-1	1931	F., 41 Housewife	Oct. 25, 1889	Twillingate, Newfoundland	Venus Jupiter Uranus Mercury	Norseland Promised Land (?) Egypt Peru
444-1	1933	F., 43 Artist, M.D. (Psychiatrist)	May 14, 1890	New York City, N.Y.	Venus Uranus Jupiter (?)	America Germany Egypt Atlantis
500-1	1934	F., 35 Naturopath	July 26, 1898	Redlands, Calif.	Mercury Jupiter Venus	America from England Persia from Egypt Egypt from Atlantis
560-1	1931	F., 45	April 7, 1886	Hull, England	Pisces Mercury Venus Jupiter Uranus	America (Virginia) England Palestine Persia Egypt

APPENDIX C

This Psychic Reading given by Edgar Cayce at his home on Arctic Crescent, Virginia Beach, Va., this 2nd day of November, 1937, in accordance with request made by the self—Mrs. [987], Associate Member of the Association for Research and Enlightenment, Inc. *Present:* Edgar Cayce; Gertrude Cayce, Conductor; Gladys Davis, Steno.; Mrs. [987].

READING

Mrs. Cayce: You will have before you the entity [987], present in this room, who seeks a Mental and Spiritual Reading, with information, advice and guidance as to her development and proper expression in the earth. You will answer the questions she submits, as I ask them:

Mr. Cayce: Yes, we have the entity, [987].

In giving the analysis of the mental and spiritual self, many are the conditions that arise as questions in the experience of the entity. These to be sure must be approached as to the purpose and the desires of the *spiritual* self.

That there may be a more perfect understanding, much as to those that have been the experiences of the entity as a soul-entity must be referred to.

For, life—or the motivative force of a soul—is eternal and that portion of same that is motivated by the mental and spiritual attributes of an entity has experienced, does experience the influences that have guided or prompted same through its sojourns.

For each soul seeks expression. And as it moves through the mental associations and attributes in the surrounding environs, it gives out that which becomes either for selfish reactions of the own ego—to express—or for the I AM to be at-one with the Great I AM THAT I AM.

What meaneth these? That self is growing to that which it, the entity, the soul, is to present, as it were, to the Great I AM in those experiences when it is absent from materiality.

These become hard at times for the individual to visualize; that the mental and soul may manifest without a physical vehicle. Yet in the deeper meditation, in those experiences when those influences may arise when the spirit of the Creative Force, the universality of soul, of mind—not as material, not as judgments, not *in* time and space but *of* time and space—may become lost in the Whole, instead of the entity being lost in the maze of confusing influences—then the soul visions arise in the meditations.

And the centers becoming attuned to the vibrations of the bodily force, these give a vision of that as may be to the entity an outlet for the self-expressions, in the beauties and the harmonies and the activities that become, in their last analysis: just being patient, long-suffering, gentle, kind. *These* are the fruits of the spirit of truth; just as hates, malice and the like become in their growths those destructive forces in creating, in making for those things that are as but tares, confusions, dissensions in the experiences of an entity.

Those then are the purposes of the entrance of an entity into a material plane; to choose that which is its ideal.

Then ask thyself the question—gain the answer first in thy physical consciousness:

"What is my ideal of a *spiritual* life?"

Then when the answer has come—for it has been given by Him that is Life, that the kingdom of God, the kingdom of heaven, is within; and we view the kingdom of God without by the application of those things that are of the spirit of truth—These then answered, ye seek again in the inner consciousness:

"Am I true to my ideal?"

These become then the answers. This and that and the other; never as pro and con. For the growth in the spirit is as He has given; ye *grow* in grace, in knowledge, in understanding.

How? As ye would have mercy shown thee, ye show mercy to those that even despitefully use thee. If ye would be forgiven for that which is contrary to thy own purposes—yet through the vicissitudes of the experiences about thee, anger and wrath give place to better judgment—ye, too, will forgive those that have despitefully used thee; ye will hold no malice. For ye would that thy Ideal, that Way ye seek, hold no malice—yea, no judgment—against thee. For it is the true law of recompense; yea, the true law of sacrifice.

For not in sacrifice alone has He sought His judgments, but rather in mercy, in grace, in fortitude; yea, in divine love.

The shadows of these are seen in thy inner experience with thy fellow man day by day. For ye have seen a smile, yea, a kind word, turn away wrath. Ye have seen a gentleness give hope to those that have lost their hold on purpose, other than the satisfying of an appetite— yea, other than satisfying the desires of the carnal mind.

Hence as ye give, ye receive. For this is mercy, this is grace. This is the beauty of the inner life lived.

Know then it is not that judgment is passed here or there. For know that God looketh upon the heart and He judgeth rather the purposes, the desires, the intents.

For what seekest thou to lord (laud) in thy life? Self intent? Know ye not that it was selfishness that separated the souls from the spirit of life and light? Then only in the divine love do ye have the opportunity to become to thy fellow man a saving grace, a mercy, yea, even a savior.

For until ye have in thy own material associations known thyself to be the saving grace to someone, ye may not know even the whole mercy of the Father with the children of men.

Then it is not of rote; it is not ritual that has made for those influences in thine own experience; but in whom, in what hast thou put thy trust?

He has promised to meet thee within the temple of thine own body. For as has been given, thy body is the temple of the living God; a tabernacle, yea, for thy soul. And in the holy of holies within thine own consciousness He may walk and talk with thee.

How? How?

Is it the bringing of sacrifice? Is it the burning of incense? Is it the making of thyself of no estate?

Rather is it that ye *purpose!* For the try, the purpose of thine inner self, to *Him* is the righteousness. For He hath known all the vicissitudes of the earthly experience. He hath walked through the valley of the shadow of death. He hath seen the temptations of man from every phase that may come into thine own experience; and, yea, He hath given thee, "If ye will love me, believing I am able, I will deliver thee from that which so easily besets thee at *any* experience."

And it is thus that He stands; not as a Lord but as thy Brother, as thy Savior; that ye may know indeed the truth that gentleness, kindness, patience, brotherly love, beget—in thy heart of hearts, with Him—that peace, that harmony. Not as the world knoweth peace but as He gave: "That peace I give you; that ye may know that thy spirit, yea, thy soul, beareth witness with me that ye are mine—I am thine," even as the Father, the Son, the Holy Spirit.

Even so may thy soul, thy mind, thy body, become aware of that which renews the hope, the faith, the patience within thee.

And until ye show forth in His love that patience, ye cannot become aware of thy relationship with Him. Even as He has given, in patience ye become aware of being that soul—that seeketh the Father's house that is within even thine own consciousness.

How? How, then, may ye approach the throne?

Turn thou within. As ye meditate, give forth in thine *own* words these thoughts:

"Father, God, Maker of Heaven and Earth! I am Thine—Thou art mine! As I claim that kinship with that holy love, keep Thou me in that consciousness of Thy Presence abiding with me: that I may be that channel of blessings to others, that I may know Thy grace, Thy mercy, Thy love—even as I show such to my fellow man!"

And ye may be very sure the answer comes within.

Thus, as ye apply—the answer comes. Not—by applying—do we mean a separation from the world. For even as He, ye are *in* the world but not *of* the world. But putting away the worldly things ye take hold upon the spiritual things, knowing that the worldly are but the shadows of the real.

And thus, as ye come into the light of His countenance, it maketh thy heart glad in the consciousness of "*I am Thine—Thou art mine.*" ...

Q-3. *If possible, what can I do to finish my earth's experience in this life?*

A-3. It is ever possible. Studying to show forth the Lord's death till He comes again!

What meaneth this?

Just living those that are the fruits of the spirit; namely: peace, harmony, long-suffering, brotherly love, patience. *These,* if ye show them forth in thy life, in thy dealings with thy fellow man, grow to be what? *Truth!* In Truth ye are *free,* from what? *Earthly* toil, *earthly* cares!

These then are not just axioms, not just sayings, but *living* truths! Ye *are* happy in His *love! Hold* fast to that!

Q-4. What is holding back my spiritual development?

A-4. Nothing holding back—as has just been given—but *self.* For know, as has been given of old, "Though I take the wings of the morning in thought and fly unto the uttermost parts of the earth, Thou are there! Though I fly into the heavenly hosts, Thou art there! Though I make my bed in hell, Thou art there!"

And as He has promised, "When ye cry unto me, I will *hear*—and answer speedily."

Nothing prevents—only self. Keep self and the shadow away. Turn thy face to the light and the shadows fall behind.

Q-6. What is the meaning of the white lightning I have seen?

A-6. That awakening that is coming. More and more as the white light comes to thee, more and more will there be the awakening. For as the lights are in the colors: In the green, healing; in the blue, trust; in the purple, strength; in the white, the light of the throne of mercy itself. Ye may never see these save ye have withheld judgment or shown mercy.

Q-7. What is my worst fault?

A-7. What is ever the worst fault of each soul? *Self—self!*

What is the meaning of self?

That the hurts, the hindrances are hurts to the self-consciousness; and these create what? Disturbing forces, and these bring about confusions and faults of every nature.

For the only sin of man is *selfishness!*

Q-8. How may it be overcome?

A-8. Just as has been given; showing mercy, showing grace, showing peace, long-suffering, brotherly love, kindness—even under the most *trying* circumstances.

For what is the gain if ye love those *only* that love thee? But to bring hope, to bring cheer, to bring joy, yea, to bring a smile again to those whose face and heart are bathed in tears and in woe, is but making that divine love *shine—shine*—in thy own soul!

Then *smile,* be joyous, be glad! For the day of the Lord is at hand. Who is thy Lord? Who is thy God?

Self? Or Him in Whom ye live and move and have thy being—that is ALL in All, God the Father, the Love—the *Great* Hope, the Great Patience?

These are thy *all.*

Keep in the way that is arising before thee, more and more. And as ye open thy consciousness to the Great Consciousness within, there will arise more and more the white light.

For He is the light, and the life—eternal.   987-4

THE EDGAR CAYCE LEGACIES

Among the vast resources which have grown out of the late Edgar Cayce's work are:

The Readings: Available for examination and study at the Association for Research and Enlightenment, Inc.,(A.R.E.®) at Virginia Beach, Va., are 14,256 readings consisting of 49,135 pages of verbatim psychic material plus related correspondence. The readings are the clairvoyant discourses given by Cayce while he was in a self-induced hypnotic sleep-state. These discourses were recorded in shorthand and then typed. Copious indexing and cross-indexing make the readings readily accessible for study.

Research and Information: Medical information which flowed through Cayce is being researched and applied by the research divisions of the Edgar Cayce Foundation. Work is also being done with dreams and other aspects of ESP. Much information is disseminated through the A.R.E. Press publications, *A.R.E. News* and *The A.R.E. Journal.* Coordination of a nationwide program of lectures and conferences is in the hands of the Department of Education. A library specializing in psychic literature is available to the public with books on loan to members. An extensive tape library has A.R.E. lectures available for purchase. Resource material has been made available for authors, resulting in the publication of scores of books, booklets and other material.

A.R.E. Study Groups: The Edgar Cayce material is most valuable when worked with in an A.R.E. Study Group, the text for which is *A Search for God,* Books I and II. These books are the outcome of eleven years of work by Edgar Cayce with the first A.R.E. group and represent the distillation of wisdom which flowed through him in the trance condition. Hundreds of A.R.E. groups flourish throughout the United States and other countries. Their primary purpose is to assist the members to know their relationship to their Creator and to become channels of love and service to others. The groups are nondenominational and avoid ritual and dogma. There are no dues or fees required to join a group although contributions may be accepted.

Membership: A.R.E. has an open-membership policy which offers attractive benefits.

For more information write A.R.E., Box 595, Virginia Beach, Va. 23451. To obtain information about publications, please direct your query to A.R.E. Press. To obtain information about joining or perhaps starting an A.R.E. Study Group, please direct your letter to the Study Group Department.